A Guide to Teaching International Students

A Guide to Teaching International Students

Janette Ryan

© Oxford Centre for Staff and Learning Development 2000

Published by
THE OXFORD CENTRE FOR STAFF AND LEARNING DEVELOPMENT
Oxford Brookes University
Gipsy Lane
Headington
Oxford
OX3 0BP

A Guide to Teaching International Students
ISBN 1 873576 65 X

British Library Cataloguing-in-Publication Data.
A catalogue record for this book is available from the British Library.

Designed and typeset in Palatino and Helvetica by Meg Richardson.

Printed in Great Britain by
Oxonian Rewley Press Ltd.
Oxford

Printed on paper produced from sustainable forests.

Contents

Acknowledgments:

Many people have contributed their time and examples of their work in the development of this Guide. Thanks are due to staff at Oxford Brookes University including Diane Seymour, Lynn Errey, Mark Ames, Liz Doherty, David Bowie, Sue Ledwith, Frank Ultsch, Glauco De Vita, Vic Truesdale and Paul Richardson. Thanks also to staff at Leeds University including Hywel Coleman, John Uren, Dick Killington, Angie Malderez, Martin Wedell, and especially to Christine Talbot for her help and support. Also to David Lippiatt at the University of Lincolnshire and Humberside, Claire Pickles at Bradford University, Keith Silvester at The Central School of Speech and Drama, Lorraine Stefani at the University of Strathclyde, Jean Roebuck at Manchester Metropolitan University, David Killick at Leeds Metropolitan University, Sarah Huws-Davies at the University of Wales, Christine Asmar at the University of Sydney, and Patricia Cartwright at Australian Catholic University. Special thanks to Mark Ames and Diane Seymour for reading the manuscript and providing invaluable comments, and heartfelt thanks to Lynn Errey for her editorial assistance. Jude Carroll of the Oxford Centre for Staff and Learning Development at Oxford Brookes University deserves very special mention for her unfailing guidance and support throughout this project, and for its original inspiration.

Introduction

1

1.1 Who this guide is for

This guide is for teaching staff who wish to improve their skills in teaching international students, who recognise that the first step towards this is to review their teaching practices and examine their own cultural values and practices, and who are prepared to change some of what they currently do or believe. It will assist you in:

- valuing the diversity of your student population;
- understanding the importance of cross-cultural knowledge and understanding; and
- improving your ability to interact with people from culturally diverse backgrounds.

It is primarily aimed at assisting staff who are working with international students in mainstream university courses, rather than in customised courses, where it is much easier to tailor course content and design for specific needs. It should be recognised that the suggestions contained in this guide will have application for a range of students with extra needs, not just international students.

An important note of caution in using this guide is that international students should be considered as individuals; assumptions cannot be made because someone belongs to a particular cultural group. The guide does give indications of the kinds of issues which may pertain for certain cultural groups, but these should always be tested to see if they are relevant to individuals within that group. These issues may be different for different groups, but whether these are students for whom English is not their first language, students from Confucian-heritage cultures, students from more collectivist or 'convergent' traditions, or students from other Western countries, most of the good practice suggestions provided in this guide are aimed at providing better teaching and learning environments for all international students, and for all students generally.

Each section within this guide gives a general discussion of the issues involved in a number of problematic areas, and then suggestions for tackling these issues are developed. At the end of each section, a number of bullet points are given that act as summaries. These summaries can also then be used as a later 'quick reference' guide.

Before you think about what changes to make, ask yourself:

- Are you aware of others' cultural biases and assumptions?

- Can you identify your own cultural biases and assumptions in an academic context?

- Do you think it is important to respect the backgrounds and values of others?

- Can you see the benefits of learning from international students?

- Are you prepared to explore ways of changing your teaching and learning practices?

- Do you think it is important to provide better learning experiences and improved outcomes for international students?

1.2 Being realistic

You don't have to change your teaching style completely to accommodate international students but you may have to make different choices as a teacher, such as what to include in subject matter and classroom tasks. You need to be culturally sensitive when you are making these choices. It is not a question of lowering standards, or of doing more. It is about doing things differently. Take a step back and look at how you can change your practices. Start small, making changes with which you feel comfortable. Remember that home students have needs as well and these should be balanced with the needs of international students, as well as your own needs.

It should be remembered however that all students, whatever their backgrounds, use the same cognitive processes and they all arrive at university with strategies for learning which they have developed in order to be successful in their previous educational institution. All students need help in adjusting to their new learning environments, not just international students.

1.3 Setting the scene for changing your teaching

Universities need to respond to the needs of international students by opening not just their doors to them, but once in, making sure that the curriculum is also accessible. International students are too often seen as a 'problem' that needs 'solving'. Instead, they should be seen as one group among many in an increasingly diverse student population with needs that may be unfamiliar. Instead of expecting all students to fit in to pre-existing structures, universities need to change the way that they respond to diverse student populations, including international students.

Teachers are often unaware that students bring unfamiliar interpretations to the learning situation. To make a difference, teachers need to appreciate that students have different cultural ways of conceptualising knowledge and that this can be expressed in unfamiliar approaches to critical thinking and writing. How might we accommodate differences without trying to change them? Teaching staff need to assist students to adapt to new environments and expectations, without seeking to transform them. If you have been raised in a Western academic tradition, it is hard to believe that, for example, the rules of essay writing that we unthinkingly accept, may be as arbitrary and culture-bound as those of the academic traditions that international students may bring to a British university.

In order to be culturally sensitive, you need to learn to be an 'anthropologist' of your own culture. This means that sometimes you will need to step back from your own cultural expectations, to consider the differences of another cultural dimension and explore the world of the international student. It means trying not only to tolerate differences, but responding positively to them, rather like trying exotic foods on the menu on an overseas holiday, not just searching for the familiar egg and chips. It also means working with your international students as individuals from a range of cultural backgrounds, and not just accepting the many stereotypes of international students that exist.

1.4   The role of culture in learning

We are continuously being constructed by our culture as part of an invisible process that goes on throughout our lives. Our cultural beliefs and practices seem so natural and familiar to us that when others exhibit culturally unexpected behaviours or beliefs, we can find these behaviours very confronting, or difficult to understand, and make negative judgements about them. When international students enter a new culture, i.e. British universities, they intuitively try to understand its rules and mores, but often only become aware of the rules when they have 'broken' them. For example, an American student, speaking loudly and proudly of his or her past achievements in a tutorial might sense some hostility to their contribution and only in time pick up the 'rules' against boasting that many British students follow. Nothing is made explicit to such a student. But a teacher can help by being culturally aware. If teachers examine their own cultural beliefs and assumptions, they may begin to understand the cultural uncertainties that international students may be experiencing when they are teaching them.

How far should we push the 'rightness' of our own culture in an academic environment? Hofstede (1991), who is a widely recognised expert in the field of cross-cultural communication, describes culture as mental programming. 'The sources of one's mental programs lie within the social environments in which one grew up and collected one's life experiences.' He argues that culture deals with more than art, education and literature but also with the 'ordinary and menial things in life' such as greeting, eating, showing or not showing feelings, keeping a certain distance from others; it deals with 'the things that hurt' and offers culturally specific ways of handling or ameliorating them. 'Culture', he states, 'is learned, not inherited. It derives from one's social environment, not from one's genes.'

It would seem that how people react to different values depends on their tolerance for difference. It is their own built-in degree of sensitivity that determines how far they can understand the underlying intentions and motivations of others. How they will see things will also depend on the implicit values prevailing in their home society and how distant these are from those they are witnessing.

With this in mind, dealing skilfully with international students needs to start with being self-aware and knowing your own cultural values better. Without becoming tuned into your own cultural values and biases, you may without knowing it make international students feel unimportant and ignored, or even discriminated against. In turn, your students may get 'stuck', unable to connect with what you are trying to teach them. When this happens, it might become impossible for them to be able to construct new knowledge and critical understandings from your teaching, and from the learning environment.

1.5   Benefits of international students

International students bring many benefits to Higher Education institutions. They enrich the cultural and intellectual environment of a university and its locality, stimulate new curriculum approaches and foster new understanding between cultures. (CVCP Briefing Note on International Students in UK Higher Education, July 1998)

Clearly UK universities are benefiting from the increase in the numbers of international students; but are there benefits to home students as well? The answer is a resounding 'yes' although young British students may not share this view. Many 18–22 year olds, away from home for the first time, often don't see the need for intercultural competence as a transferable skill in their future professions. Many UK students do not realise the advantages of going to an 'international' university. In 1995/96, 22,000 EU students attended UK universities, yet less than half of that number of British students went to EU universities. International students could and indeed should be seen as an asset to universities, as bearers of culture, as living resources to assist students to learn intercultural skills and sensitivity. Sadly, they are not always viewed so positively.

1.6   Difficulties of UK/international student contacts

Ledwith et al. (1998) reported findings from their research that home students often resented working in groups with international students (see also Working in groups, Chapter 3, section 3.8, below) and international students themselves reported that one of their most significant problems was establishing and maintaining relationships with home students. International students reported that they found home students to be self-centred, overly-competitive and sometimes discriminatory, while home students saw international students as under-confident and overly-quiet. These stereotypes arise from a mismatch of cultural perceptions.

In 1996/97, international students in UK Higher Education institutions:

- *totalled 198,000*

- *comprised 11 per cent of full-time undergraduate students and 34 per cent of postgraduates*

- *43 per cent were from the EU, and 28 per cent from Asia*

- *contributed (in 1995/96) £750m to the UK economy and £600m in fees*

(CVCP Briefing note)

Teachers are the ones who can make a difference in establishing the learning environments and expectations of their students. Their classroom behaviour can set the tone for how the attitudes and contributions of others are viewed. If they do not, for example, challenge racist remarks or jokes, they are sending an implicit message that those kinds of behaviours are acceptable. Rather than expecting home students to change, teachers should provide a teaching environment that explicitly values differences. Such a positive environment will provide opportunities for international students to demonstrate and share their knowledge. In this way, home students will also learn to appreciate the experiences of others and broaden their own perspectives.

1.7 Teachers' concerns

Behind the comments made by teachers, it is clear that they often feel a resentment towards what they perceive to be international students' lack of intellectual independence. They may not understand that international students may be merely exhibiting learning strategies that were expected of them in their previous learning, strategies which at the time were rewarded. For example, international students may not initially be prepared to deal with the autonomous learning style common to Western education, with less contact time and less guidance. Teachers can be resentful where international students appear more demanding, lacking in computer, library or laboratory skills, have different and unfamiliar modes of behaviour and expression, seem to use only descriptive rather than analytic approaches to learning, and bring a different dynamic to the classroom. Teachers also sometimes resent having to assess pages and pages of what they consider to be unreadable English. They may consider international students to be a burden on their time and efforts, for which they receive no reward or career advantage.

Sometimes I think international students take so much of my time, but then I realise that this is not that dissimilar to teaching mature age students, students who are academically underprepared, or some of the younger students who come to university with little life experience to draw on. The real problem is that some international students can have all of these characteristics!

(Teacher at a Northern University)

At this point there seems to be an important gap between the needs and expectations of both students and lecturers. Teachers and students both need to learn how to adapt to these new relationships and recognise that the process can involve tensions on both sides. There are no quick or easy solutions and attempts to adapt to fundamentally different expectations of relationships can be confronting and distressing. Adaptation will be slow and difficult but will be accelerated by empathy and a willingness to learn from one another. This guide is an attempt to assist in this process.

What you can do

- Recognise that we are all constructed by our culture. Like you, international students are individuals with their own set of cultural experiences and values, approaches to knowledge and learning and ways of approaching a task. All of your behaviours – yours and your students – are shaped and determined by different cultural and intellectual traditions.

- Examine the assumptions you hold about the 'ideal student' – how can you help students to be more like that without changing their current cultural behaviours? This guide will help to explain how you can do this.

Understanding approaches to knowledge and learning in different cultures

2

It is important to understand not only how culture shapes individuals, but also how it shapes cognition and learning, and what is valued as knowledge and learning within different cultures. Cultural experiences and expectations impact on the teaching and learning process, and influence the fundamental relationships in the education process, especially those between teacher and learner.

International students will often come from cultures with different:

- modes of participation, including relationships between teacher and student;
- learning styles and approaches to learning; and
- attitudes to knowledge and learning.

Although it can be dangerous to make generalisations, in broad terms, you may find that the previous learning environments of many international students (particularly those from Asian and African cultures) may be characterised by:

- a respect for historical texts and previously accumulated knowledge;
- a respect for authority figures, including teachers;
- not being overtly critical of authoritative texts or figures;
- the importance of the 'correct' answer;
- avoidance of making mistakes or losing 'face';
- expectations of listening quietly;
- personal opinions appearing arrogant;
- the importance of harmony and cooperation within the group over the interests of the individual within it.

Comments made in the following sections about learning characteristics of international students are made in terms of likely variations that may be present, and that have frequently been observed, and should be read in that context. Not all students will display the characteristics that are commonly associated with their cultural group, and some lecturers have noticed distinct changes in their students in recent years. One lecturer, for example, noted that his past Chinese (mainly women) students had been predominantly passive, but in the previous two years he had a number who were 'feisty, up-front, jokey, vociferous and demanding'.

2.1 Role of the teacher and the student

Many international students come from educational environments that are vastly different from those in the UK. Many, but not all, will experience greater or lesser difficulties in adjusting to their new environment. Different academic traditions mean that they may not only be coming with very different educational experiences, but many will have radically different expectations of how they as learners are meant to behave, as well as how teachers are meant to behave. Where two sets of expectations intersect, there will be many opportunities for misunderstandings and hurt feelings.

Hofstede (1991) argues that there are four distinct areas in which cultures vary:

1. power distance – the extent to which less powerful members of the society accept inequality of power distribution;

2. individualist / collectivist – individual: where people look after themselves and their immediate family; collectivist: where people belong to 'strong cohesive in-groups' which protect them and to which they are loyal;

3. masculinity / femininity – 'male': social gender roles are clearly defined; 'female': roles overlap;

4. uncertainty avoidance – the extent to which the members of a culture feel threatened by uncertain or unknown situations.

Ask yourself

- Using Hofstede's categories, can you identify the type of culture to which you belong?

- How do you think that these might influence your own actions as a teacher?

2.2   Impact on teacher–student relationship

In high power distance cultures, there is:

- high level of respect for teachers;
- teachers direct student learning;
- teachers are not questioned;
- students only speak in class when invited by the teacher.

In low power distance countries:

- teachers expect students to be independent and to show initiative;
- students may question and contradict the teacher;
- students can speak spontaneously in class.

'Power distance' has a strong bearing on the nature of the teacher–student relationship. Lecturers for example often report that Asian students have an 'over-regard' for the authority of lecturers and are reluctant to question a lecturer's opinions. On the other hand, Scandinavian students generally share very similar views on appropriate power distance; few lecturers cite these students as problematic.

2.3   Impact on students' perceptions of themselves

Difference between individualistic and collectivist societies is shown by how individuals within those societies see themselves – as independent beings or interdependent ones. In a learning situation, for example, a person's own perceived role as a student will influence how they will approach teachers and fellow students. International students will often come from (in Hofstede's terms) more 'masculine' societies where there is a strong 'uncertainty avoidance', that is, where relationships are hierarchical and clearly defined. This is often displayed by students being overly deferential to teachers or by their reluctance to address teachers by their first names.

Most international students therefore have clear expectations about their own role and that of the teacher. When these expectations are not met, students may complain about lack of personal attention and commitment, or feel that they have been given little feedback on work they have laboured over. In previous schooling, they perhaps experienced higher levels of personal support and interaction with teachers, and extensive feedback and assistance with assessment tasks. However, they may see the relationship as very much a two-way

Back home I always had my family to support me and give me encouragement, and my teachers helped me with each step of my study. Here I don't have those kinds of support so I have to turn to my compatriots for help. We talk about things and help one another understand what we need to do.

(Student from Asia)

exchange. In return for more attention, they will highly revere teachers and regard them as very knowledgeable. On the other hand, other international students may bring the opposite expectations to the classroom. Some European students on ERASMUS exchanges find that the UK higher education system is too rigid, formal and constraining of activity, compared to what they have been used to.

Most international students know what they want: empathy and coaching. They want to learn to be successful as students. But they also expect teachers to be able to support them, in learning the new skills required of them. In the absence of support from teachers, students have to find alternative means of support quickly, and will often turn to other students from their own culture, in order to establish peer support mechanisms.

2.4 Collaborative learning

International students, especially those from collectivist societies, tend to form study groups to work together to understand lecture notes and to work on assignments. This can sometimes be seen as cheating or 'syndication' especially if assignments produced are similar. Yet teachers themselves often seem to require this type of behaviour when they set group tasks, and international students can be confused by apparent mixed messages. Many international students view this type of collaborative working as a valuable form of learning, providing mutual support which draws on their collectivist traditions.

2.5 Learning styles and approaches

Although superficially the problems that international students experience appear to stem from poor English skills, it is more likely that they are the result of students having to adapt rapidly to many factors in the new environment. In their steep learning curve, they also need to assimilate new attitudes to knowledge and approaches to learning.

At the beginning of their overseas studies, international students from many countries may often be academically under-prepared, they may lack relevant background knowledge only accessible to those within the English speaking culture, and be accustomed to different teaching and learning approaches. This can lead to unrealistic perceptions of their ability to undertake advanced academic work in an English language medium. Teachers may assume that international students have a similar 'general knowledge' in the discipline area as home students. International students can become demoralised by early study experiences and even resentful of staff. They can lose confidence, especially if they realise that their writing skills in the discipline are inadequate. Some may become overloaded by their attempts to read course materials and background information. In addition, they may be mystified by new concepts and expectations such as independent study, 'critical thinking' and plagiarism. Most will become distressed if their attempts to master these new skills are unsuccessful.

Many staff are not aware of these feelings commonly felt by newly arrived international students. Barker (in McNamara and Harris 1997) recounts what he discovered when he tried to find out students' early reactions:

> To be thrust suddenly into situations where they were expected to interact, debate, find out information for themselves, and critically assess it was bewildering. They felt that it was the responsibility of teaching staff to ease them gradually into this way of learning. Lack of constructive feedback on performance left students uncertain how to improve, particularly in the analysis of material and in written expression. They felt that they did not receive enough advice on study skills to help them to make the transition to self-responsibility and self-directed learning. They considered too that teaching staff did not really understand the difficulties of listening and writing in a foreign language.

The major problems for international students in the curriculum often come from the different academic training they have received. They may be unfamiliar with the critical, more active and engaged role required and are sometimes unaware that lecturers, or texts, can be questioned and challenged. Students from collectivist cultures may have been taught that personal opinion is the height of arrogance and that their role as students is to accumulate the knowledge of those wiser than them. Chinese learners for example generally believe that success comes through hard work rather than innate ability.

2.6 'Convergent' versus 'divergent' academic approaches

For many students, especially those from non-European 'convergent' cultures, the teaching and learning traditions in regard to academic writing, research and assessment are very different from those of the 'divergent' western model. Their past training and experience will have given them a very different idea of what it takes to be a 'good' student; for instance they may be accustomed to being rewarded for 'following the master' rather than 'questioning the question'. A written product based on these ways of working can be wrongly assessed as plagiarism and an inability to think analytically. Students find themselves inexplicably penalised in their work for behaviour for which they have been previously rewarded. It does not help when an essay topic is ambiguous, or so open-ended that students are unsure how to tackle it. Students may not even be aware that there are a number of possible ways to interpret and react to the statements made in essay topics, or that it is possible openly to challenge these given statements. In addition, the types and structure of arguments they have been taught in their home country may be very different from the classic Aristotelian method favoured in Western universities, so that a Western lecturer, meeting an unfamiliar structure, may find it incoherent, and reject it as having little value.

2.7 Different approaches to knowledge and learning

Cultural backgrounds and experience shape not only learning development, but also determine what we value as knowledge and learning.

Richardson (1994) states that approaches to learning vary systematically from one culture to another. He found that all systems of higher education documented as their aims the two distinct approaches towards knowledge: a transformative orientation and a reproductive one. He found however that the tendency towards the reproductive approach varied across cultures.

Students from Asian cultures are generally portrayed as having a more 'conserving' attitude to knowledge than an 'extending' one. Western universities generally expect students to demonstrate creative, challenging and questioning learning behaviours, whereas in Eastern societies, harmony and compromise are highly valued for survival and social well-being. Asian students may therefore tend to rely more on the work of recognised 'sages' in constructing their arguments in essays, rather than seek to quote from newer, less well-known authors who may seem to be espousing radical or unfamiliar ideas.

Although clear differences in attitudes to knowledge and approaches to study do exist across cultures, it is important to recognise that we may be creating inaccurate stereotypes. This is not helpful and may act as a barrier to the successful teaching of international students. To avoid stereotypes, we must look more closely at 'quick' assumptions.

2.8 Sorting out fact from assumptions about international students

What is the result of stereotyping a student? Although we may note clear observable differences in the learning approaches of international students, overstating differences can lead to such students' skills and abilities being underestimated, and their learning being unfairly viewed as 'problematic'. Differences in the learning approaches of international students should be understood as resulting from valid formative experience. If the teacher sees the student producing something that looks like 'rote learning', or is written in poor English, there is a chance for reflection: ask yourself how the student can be 'scaffolded' in their initiation into local academic requirements.

Recent researchers have questioned this conventional wisdom that Asian students are rote learners and adopt superficial learning strategies (Kember and Gow, 1991; O'Donoghue, 1996). They suggest that close memorisation is regarded as the path to deeper understanding of the material being studied. These approaches can produce results which are just as good.

Recent research (Kember and Gow, 1991) has also shown that learning approaches of students are heavily influenced by teaching and learning environments and approaches, and the nature of the curriculum, rather than inherent characteristics of students. These researchers argue that students adopt 'deep', 'surface' or 'strategic' approaches to study according to the teaching and learning approaches of the country in which they are studying. The documented learning goals of higher education systems are very similar across cultures. Where reproductive learning is evident, however, it can be due to either overloaded curricula or inappropriate assessment strategies. International students therefore need time to adapt to new approaches.

The stress involved in being an international student may also result in students' taking a more superficial or pragmatic approach than they have done previously. Students can adopt a surface approach to learning when they become overloaded with work or when assessment methods require recall of information.

O'Donoghue (1996) states:

those who promote such a view [of Asian learners] and encourage the students to reject what is perceived to be rote learning may be doing them a disservice. This contention arises out of the recent work of Watkins (1993) which suggests that students at least from Hong Kong, China and Japan are, when engaged in what Westerners perceive to be rote learning, actually weaving memorising and understanding in ways not normally found in Western learners.

17

2.9 Helping students to adapt their learning strategies

To be successful in their new environments, international students need to be aware of the learning strategies expected of them. They need to receive explicit training in how to adapt to transformative approaches to learning and knowledge and how to operate more successfully where there are more innovative teaching modes.

2.9.1 What students can do

International students (particularly non-Western students) may need training to adapt their own learning styles. It may be useful for them initially to try to assess their own approaches to learning (by for example working with staff in language centres or a study skills adviser) and working towards adapting these to their new learning environment.

Alternatively students often find some of the self-diagnostic study skills information available on the Internet useful (many of which use instruments such as the Myer-Briggs personality quiz). By identifying their own learning behaviours and preferences, they can work towards maximising their strengths and identifying those areas they need to work on. Some useful sites can be found at the addresses given in Table 2.1.

Table 2.1
Self-diagnostic study skills information: useful Internet sites

---

What is your personal learning style
http://www.howtolearn.com/personal.html

Assessing your learning style:
auditory-visual-tactile/kinaesthetic
http://www.fln.vcu.edu/Intensive/Avstyle.html

Multiple intelligence theory
http://www.scbe.on.ca/mit/mi.htm#ICO

Learning styles links
http://snow.utoronto.ca/Learn2/introll.html

2.9.2 What teachers can do

- Match the learning tasks you set to students' learning styles and preferences – use students' own cultural learning approaches to achieve learning outcomes, such as small-group collaborative tasks.

- Where students are used to a 'deep' approach to learning, it may be preferable initially to use a limited number of texts and require students to study these in depth, rather than using an extensive list and expecting students to scan-read them; or offer students the choice of which method they would like to use.

- Allow (and facilitate) study methods that take advantage of students' own approaches to learning, e.g. establishing peer study groups for study and essay writing.

- Encourage native tongue discussion groups for group discussion, shared reading and discussion of materials, arguing and sharing opinions, and clarifying confusions (but ensure that students are aware of the risks of syndication if they jointly work on assessment tasks).

2.10 Valuing difference

International students coming into a new learning environment are bound to expect certain changes and new experiences. However, they may arrive at a point where they ask themselves how far they should be prepared to change, or give up beliefs and values, to conform to lecturers' expectations.

Taking the view that international students should change to suit their new environment could be seen as unwarranted interference in the lives of international students and even as a form of cultural imperialism, and may simply not be possible for some students to achieve.

A Middle Eastern student at a university in the north of England commented to her supervisor that as she had undergone such a change in her personality and appearance during her studies, such as dying her hair red, she could not possibly return to her homeland as she would no longer be accepted.

Cortazzi and Jin (1997) argue:

> Since cultures carry with them principles and systems of
> interpretation, the potential solution of simply asking overseas
> students to assimilate to British ways is unlikely to be successful
> since these aspects of culture are deep-rooted and change may be
> seen as a threat to identity ... The basic need is for participants in
> higher education to be aware of the kinds of cultural variations in
> communication and learning which can lead to different
> understandings. This means that both teachers and students need
> awareness of how to interpret others' words and to be sensitive to
> ways in which their own words might be interpreted ... they
> [international students] will inevitably move towards British
> academic ways, but without losing their own. When they see
> tutors making efforts to understand them in their own terms they
> will realise there is no threat to their cultural identity but rather
> the opportunity to enlarge their cultural repertoire of strategies ...
> Like the students, tutors do not need to surrender their own
> (British) academic ways, but can only gain by understanding
> others' ways. Arguably, to understand alternative approaches and
> interpretations is at the heart of academic endeavour (in one's
> own subject matter).

Teachers need to make clear through their words and actions that
students' own cultural values and previous educational traditions are
not being challenged or derided. Their differing discourse patterns,
such as rhetorical structures, or self-effacing style of conversation, are
different but not of lesser value. They need to be shown that their
behaviours are respected and not considered odd or inferior.
Sometimes however international students willingly put themselves
through an entire change of culture, personality and appearance
during their studies and welcome the new academic environment.

Ask yourself

- What am I trying to achieve with my international students: to help them to master the discipline or to train them to master the discipline in the 'British way'?

Operating effectively as a teacher of international students

3

3.1 Inclusive teaching practices

The sections below refer to particular methods and strategies that you can use to assist international students in particular teaching situations. However, your own personal approach and cultural self-awareness also impact on all aspects of your teaching and learning practices in a broader sense. For example, you can make a difference by the language you use, your communication style, how you choose to respond to racist or derogatory remarks in class, and whether you include students in decisions about what you teach and assess.

3.2 Your own use of language

> By using language with care you can embrace your varied audience rather than unthinkingly alienate parts of it (Open University's Guide to Language and Image, 1993)

The use of particular words or ways of expressing terms can unwittingly cause offence to some groups of international students and can make them feel excluded. Here are some suggestions to avoid this.

- Avoid using terms such as 'our culture' – this can imply that other cultures are regarded as inferior or irrelevant.

- Avoid terms such as 'third world' or 'underdeveloped countries' which also imply inferiority – even 'joking' terms are usually unwelcome, e.g. 'Antipodean' offends many Australians.

- Use respectful terms – 'an Asian student' highlights cultural difference, but 'a student from Singapore' acknowledges the person as an individual.

- Only use additional information about students, such as religious, racial or national descriptors, when it is relevant.

- When describing other cultural practices and religions, try to do this accurately and not in a sensational way; look for common features as well as different ones.

- Do not refer to other cultural or religious practices and beliefs as myths, legends or superstitions. Affording your own beliefs and practices higher status and respect displays a form of cultural imperialism and can be deeply offensive to those who hold different beliefs.

- Do not assume that all students coming from a particular cultural group will be the same, or expect them to speak on behalf of the entire group; recognise the heterogeneity of international students and the multi-faceted characteristics of individual students.

3.3 Responding to racist remarks

Racist remarks and jokes in class can cause deep offence to international students and should always be challenged. You can state in course handbooks, or in an early discussion of ground rules for the class, that racist (and sexist or homophobic) comments and jokes are not permitted.

Work out in advance what strategies you will take in responding to such remarks in class. These will vary according to the context of the comment and how comfortable you feel about different ways of responding.

You can overtly challenge such remarks, and correct the comments made, or you can make it clear that you consider the comment inappropriate by making an obvious pause, and then asking the student to justify their statement. You don't necessarily have to engage in an argument about the comment, but you could open the issue up for discussion by asking other students for their reactions, and turn the situation into a learning opportunity.

- Always respond to racist or offensive remarks.

- Work out your responses in advance.

- Make it clear that such remarks are unacceptable.

- Explicitly state in course materials that racism will not be tolerated.

3.4 Consult with students

The best way to ensure that you are responding to the needs of international students is by consulting with them and asking if they feel that their needs are being met or if they have any suggestions for areas that they would like you to cover. This can be done either informally on a one-to-one basis, or with small groups, or it can be done formally with a selection of international students periodically invited to address course or staff meetings.

At the University of Michigan's Center for Research on Learning and Teaching and the University of Massachusetts's Center for Teaching, orientation programmes for new faculty members include sessions where a panel of students from diverse backgrounds talk about how teachers can help them to learn.

> Not only does this session provide tips for new teachers, it also serves as a reminder in our large institutions that the sea of student faces is composed of individuals with myriad perspectives and needs (Ewing Cook and Sorcinelli, 1999).

3.5 How inclusive are you?

- Are you assisting international students to achieve their full potential? Are they able to fully participate in the curriculum?

- Do you attempt to ensure that international students are provided with a sympathetic learning environment where they feel safe to contribute their ideas?

3.6 Lectures

The format of formal lectures can pose major problems for international students. They may not understand the conventions and discourse structures of lectures, and intelligibility of individual lectures may prove difficult for them. The student may have problems but it is the lecturer's responsibility to ensure the lecture is understood by students.

The nature of lectures means that, unlike face-to-face communication, students' levels of comprehension cannot be checked. Intelligibility of lectures can be influenced by speed of delivery, accent, use of unfamiliar grammatical structures, vocabulary, idioms, sentence length, sequencing, predictability and by whether or not students can see and interpret facial expressions and gestures. International students may not be able to interpret verbal and physical gestures signalling important information in lectures. In addition, the English language is very dependent on the stress placed on individual words within a sentence in order to understand its meaning.

There are many strategies that lecturers can employ to assist international students to comprehend and make better sense of lectures. Many of these strategies will help other groups of students as well.

3.6.1 Organisation

- Provide an overall context at the start of a lecture including important necessary background information so that students can make connections with previous knowledge and experiences to facilitate deeper learning.

- Briefly go over the main points of the previous lecture and link them to the current lecture, showing relevance and sequence.

- Explain the structure of the lecture as well as its main points.

- Take students through the construction of a lecture as an example of how arguments are constructed.

- Provide an outline of the lecture for students to take away.

- Explain key concepts, assuming no background knowledge.

- Provide copies of your lecture notes.

- Make sure that handouts are sufficiently clear and are not just acting as reminders to already able students.

- Permit lectures to be taped.

- Define any jargon or unknown words.

- Spell out acronyms and abbreviations.

I encourage international students to tape-record their lectures, but ask them to use these to take notes from and then erase the tapes, rather then just storing them.

(Lecturer, Bradford University)

- Write out proper names, new words or phrases, technical or difficult words.

- Do not talk while you are writing.

- Allow time for students to take down the information.

- Try to alleviate the strain of continuous listening for long periods by changing activities and having short pauses.

- Summarise the key points at the end of each section, clearly and slowly, and link ideas.

- Repeat and summarise throughout.

- Provide a short summary at the end of the lecture.

- Provide one or two readings for the next lecture (ensure that these are suitable for beginning students).

3.6.2 Your language

- At the start of the lecture, restrict vocabulary and sentence structure to simple, easily understood ones and gradually increase complexity; when you introduce a complex or more sophisticated word or structure, repeat it using a more simple alternative to aid comprehension.

- Keep sentences short and clearly order sentence parts.

- Use measured, clear speech, especially to indicate main points.

- Use the active voice.

- Use 'international' English, i.e. simplified and everyday words; the most commonly used forms and vocabulary.

- Finish the ends of your words.

- Repeat important statements.

- Insert pauses.

- Avoid redundancy of language.

- Link ideas.

- Allow students to 'side-talk' to each other – this aids comprehension.

I hand out a short questionnaire or quiz at the end of the lecture to check if the main points were understood. I then cover areas that were not well understood in the next lecture or invite students to follow these issues up in a tutorial.

(Lecturer, Oxford Brookes University)

25

3.6.3 Non-verbal props

- Try to give a visual picture of the lecture structure and content.

- Use a variety of teaching aids which also give visual clues; use concept maps, diagrams, pictures, cartoons.

- When using visual materials, ensure they are clear and unambiguous.

- If using cartoons or pictures, make sure that they can be understood across cultures or provide an explanation.

3.6.4 Signposting

- Use explicit verbal markers to indicate important information (e.g. 'This last point is very important', 'In conclusion', 'And now we'll look at a few examples of this') and implicit ones (loudness, stress, repetition using alternative words or phrases, sentence length) to aid comprehension.

- Provide verbal and physical signals to indicate transitions from one idea to another, e.g. 'And then we move on to the next major issue …'

3.6.5 Readings

- Indicate essential texts.

- Make it clear you expect students to read selectively.

- Indicate where lecture material relates to particular sections of textbooks or other materials so that students can do supplementary reading.

3.6.6 Afterwards

- Indicate clearly that it is normal that everything covered may not be understood fully and that it is legitimate to seek extra help and clarification.

- Invite students to use email to ask questions; use subject web pages to post responses for all students to see.

- Be available for a few minutes before and after lectures – some international students are more accustomed to being able to ask questions individually after class.

Some lecturers put their lecture notes on the University's internal website so that students can download them after the lecture and have more time to understand them.

(Bradford University)

3.6.7 Things to avoid

- Be especially careful in the use of humour; unless it can be understood by all students, it can make some students feel excluded and may be deeply offensive to some groups of students if the subject matter is sensitive.

- Avoid comments that may be construed as sexist, racist, homophobic or offensive to particular groups.

- Do not use case studies or examples that only home students can understand such as football or breweries.

- Avoid using culturally specific analogies, anecdotes, and jargon that can only be understood by British students, e.g. references to 'Dickensian characters'.

Ask yourself

- Is a mass lecture the most appropriate method to teach this topic?

- Does your decision to lecture pose difficulties for international students (and other students such as disabled students) who might have difficulty with fast note-taking?

3.7 Seminars and tutorials

Successful participation in group working settings can pose many problems for international students. They will most likely be lacking in language skills, but may also lack:

- experience of participation-based learning;
- experience in class or group discussions;
- ability and skills required to read large amounts of texts;
- experience of assessed group tasks or working in groups; and
- study skills.

Participation by international students in the classroom can be inhibited by many factors such as by fear of:

- embarrassment;
- making a mistake;
- using incorrect English;
- loss of 'face';
- appearing foolish;
- wasting others' time;
- implying that the teacher has not explained well;
- appearing arrogant by expressing a personal opinion;
- showing lack of respect for the teacher by asking questions.

As with lectures, there are many strategies and interventions that teachers can use to assist international students to participate more successfully and achieve better outcomes in group working settings such as tutorials, seminars and small group work. These are set out below.

3.7.1 Lack of experience in participation-based learning

International students may not have any experience of discussion-based approaches to learning so this needs to be handled sensitively at first. The seminar or tutorial setting can cause enormous anxiety for many international students. Many factors can lead to this anxiety, such as lack of experience, lack of knowledge of Western conversation rules and norms, as well as lack of adequate language skills. International students will often respond with passivity and silence, and even sometimes withdrawal. Of course, not all of the reasons for remaining silent arise from feeling inadequate. International students will often respond 'yes' when asked whether they have understood and then ask a friend to explain. Saying no would imply that the teacher had not explained the point well, and would be insulting. Not questioning the teacher shows respect.

- Explain the purpose of seminars and tutorials (e.g. for students themselves to debate issues arising from lectures, to give the opportunity for critical analysis of major themes of the course and course materials etc.).

A Japanese student approached me saying that she could not possibly do the oral presentation task set for the unit assessment, and that she would rather fail than have to do it as she felt that her English was not good enough. I discussed several options with her and we decided that she should give the presentation individually to me. She did this and was assessed well, in fact having few problems with the language. I then gave her the option of giving the presentation to the whole class. She did this, again doing quite well. Once the situation had been 'de-stressed', she was able to perform well.

(Lecturer at an Australian university)

- Explain differences between approaches and emphases in lectures, seminars and tutorials (this will also benefit other groups of students such as first-generation university students).

- Explain 'rules' and expectations for participation in different learning formats.

- Advise topics and readings in advance so that students have time to prepare.

3.7.2 Language problems

Many international students will not want to draw attention to themselves when they do not follow what the teacher or other students are saying in class. They may feel too embarrassed to take up the time of other class members or the teacher. Silence and passivity in themselves are often seen as virtues in some cultures and individuals can find it difficult to overcome deeply ingrained cultural behaviours. It requires a high degree of language competence and understanding of the way people are expected to interact in a tutorial or seminar to be able to participate effectively. International students when faced with stressful situations, such as oral presentations, may feel that they are not yet adequately equipped to participate with dignity and without loss of face.

Language difficulties can be compounded by a huge range of factors such as nuances in meanings of words that appear to be synonyms, or obscure cultural and literary references. This can be compounded by professional jargon, the use of slang, and individual peculiarities of accent. English can be a particularly difficult, irregular, unpredictable language compared to many languages which follow ordered grammatical patterns.

- Give students prior warning the week beforehand of when they will be required to speak in class, so that they can prepare what they are going to say. Alternatively, ask them to work in pairs, so they can assist one another to report to the class.

- For oral presentations, consider where it might be possible to allow international students to videotape their presentation, or use a format that requires less talking (such as a poster presentation). Alternatively, allow them to negotiate with you another type of task if they feel that an oral presentation will seriously disadvantage them at that point in their language development.

I wanted to join in discussions like the others but used to get so nervous that my body shook. In my mind I was fully engaged in the classroom and had something to say, but feared making a fool of myself in front of the class. 'Have I understood what's been said? Is my question too obvious? Am I on the right track? Am I going to get stuck half-way? Am I going to make a grammatical error?' Usually I missed the moment and never got around to saying a word. My Thai friends were different from me in this aspect. They weren't even interested in trying to say anything. They thought speaking up or arguing with the lecturer in class was not the right behaviour.

(Nagata, 1999)

29

3.7.3 Lack of experience in class or group discussion

Many international students will find answering a question in class, or giving a presentation, an excruciating experience. They need to be eased into this at the start and especially during their first year. The teacher should construct tasks that allow them to prepare their responses in advance, or in pairs. Such activities create a safe and supportive learning environment. Even with good English language skills, some international students will not participate in group discussions if they feel unsafe or unconfident.

Female international students, in particular, may have trouble participating in class if they have come from cultures where females have been expected to show deference, not take the initiative, and speak only when spoken to. Some women however will enjoy the new opportunity to be able to speak out.

Different cultural groups have different approaches to speaking in groups. In Asian groups, the talker will avoid being explicit as this will imply that the listener is not subtle enough to work out the implications of what is being said. Students from the Middle East may talk loudly and use heavy intonation. The reply 'Yes' may have a range of meanings. There may be different rules for 'turn-taking', pauses, eye contact, physical contact or body language, and these may lead to misinterpretation by others, or poor timing for intervention.

You need to be sensitive in the ways that you respond to the contributions that international students make, and to the ways that they express these. You need to be careful in how classroom discussion takes place to ensure that international students have opportunities to make contributions. They need to be valued and responded to by other students. When you do this, you may start to find that you think carefully in advance about how you construct and manage classroom tasks and discussions where you want all students to respond. Just asking a question and waiting for responses disadvantages all kinds of students but especially international students.

3.7.4 At the beginning

- Use name tags for the first session and for introduction activities, or use some other kind of warm-up activity.

- Organise informal, non-threatening activities so students get to know one another.

When students first meet, I organise them into pairs, and ask them to find out three pieces of information about one another. I place a pack of cards into a container and ask students to select one. Students then pair with another student with the same card (e.g. two kings). They can ask each other about items such as background, why they are doing the course, their ambitions etc. After five or ten minutes, each pair briefly reports back to the class on what the other student has told them. This is an easier way for students to talk about themselves, and is less intimidating than individuals talking about themselves directly to the whole group. It also has the advantage that each student then knows at least one other student.

(Lecturer, Deakin University, Australia)

3.7.5 Encouraging participation

- Include tasks that require participation by all students.

- Initially, set very structured tasks with clear guidelines.

- Encourage international students to ask questions; make it clear that all questions are valid; encourage international students to take risks with questions, and give positive reinforcement.

- Allow a range of different types of participation.

- Use non-threatening, and non-personal, questions.

Ask yourself

- Do you provide opportunities for and safe and sympathetic learning environments for small group discussion?

- Do you construct these in ways that prevent student or teacher dominance?

- Do you set tasks that assume significant background knowledge?

3.7.6 Use of language

- Let students use their own words and ways of expressing themselves.

- Ensure that international students have opportunities to talk. Allow them more time to respond, allow more pauses for 'think time', and try to avoid the temptation of jumping in to finish their sentences. If they are struggling, suggest a word or phrase but then let them complete what they want to say.

- Do not correct the student's language overtly. You may need to rephrase the student's question or subtly use the correct words or phrases in your answer, and if necessary, help out later in private.

- If you don't understand what the student is trying to say, ask a few questions but if you still don't understand, try to avoid embarrassment for the student by suggesting you discuss the point after the class.

- When checking comprehension, avoid asking if everyone has understood (implying that they all should have). Instead try questions such as 'Is there anything that is still unclear?', 'Have I explained that well enough?', 'One or two areas may still be unclear', 'Any questions?'

- Recognise that reversion to native language is sometimes a necessary or relief mechanism.

3.7.7   Encouraging an inclusive environment

- Try to avoid always emphasising differences in cultures, try to find common characteristics and features as well.

- Do not refer to a person's race or ethnic background if it is not relevant.

- Try not only to cultivate new knowledge acquisition in students but also to foster an understanding and appreciation of differences and interpersonal understandings to create a sense of community within classrooms.

- Create opportunities for socialisation between international students and other students.

- Do not expect students to talk for their whole cultural group – for instance, avoid asking individual students for the Muslim perspective – but provide opportunities for students to contribute their cultural knowledge when they so wish.

- Encourage different types of contributions in the class and explicitly state that diverse viewpoints are valued.

- Explicitly state that racist and sexist comments or jokes are banned and that racist or sexist behaviour will not be tolerated.

- Include in the learning outcomes for the unit an awareness of cross-cultural issues relevant to the discipline.

- Recognise that working on cultural issues can be difficult and emotional.

- Try to learn about the cultures of your students and encourage them to talk about themselves, their experiences and their cultures. Don't overdo this, however, or put pressure on students to talk before they are ready

- Try to encourage home students to learn about the cultures and backgrounds of other students, and to learn how to pronounce other students' names correctly.

3.7.8 Group discussions

- In group discussions, make sure that only one student speaks at once and try to allow for pauses in between student contributions. If a native speaker makes a complex or ambiguous point, stop and discuss the point to ensure that it is understood by all. Try to encourage home students to make sure that their points are understood by everyone.

- Try to ensure that contributions made by international students lead to whole group discussion as much as contributions made by other students.

- Rather than asking individual students to respond to questions, ask students to write their responses down and discuss them with a partner before asking for responses to be shared as a group.

- Use pair work to encourage confidence and learning from a native speaker, initially only require short, safe answers.

3.7.9 Getting students to read what you want, in the way you want

The volume of reading required is a major problem for international students. They can feel overwhelmed by the choices that need to be made for reading lists and library catalogues. Many need to learn critical reading skills such as selective reading techniques and skim reading (see also Helping students to improve their study skills, section 3.9, below). You can assist in making this easier by signalling the importance of texts and helping students to read selectively and efficiently and to take notes more effectively. For example, international students are often unfamiliar with 'mining' techniques where a text is read and relevant items are lifted from the text and quoted for the relevant purpose (see also Plagiarism and syndication, Chapter 4, section 4.11, below).

I start each term with an exercise where all of the students in the tutorial have to tell their names to the rest of the class and explain how they got their name, and what it means. Of course, many home students have absolutely no idea where their name comes from, but it does make for a fun session, and students do remember everyone else's name.

(Lecturer, The Central School for Speech and Drama)

3.7.10 **Helping with reading strategies**

- On reading lists, flag up essential texts.

- Prioritise and annotate reading lists.

- Explain why texts have been chosen, how they connect with the topic, and how they conceptually connect with or challenge the topic.

- Make it clear that students should read selectively and critically.

- Help students to establish a clear purpose to their reading.

- Show previous good model essays which have used texts selectively.

- You may need to model selective and critical reading techniques such as:

  - the importance of looking at indexes, chapter headings and sub-headings, abstracts, opening and concluding points, before reading parts of the main text;

  - selecting key points and summarising;

  - questioning the viewpoint of the author and encouraging the expression of alternative viewpoints: Do the students identify with the author's viewpoint or are their experiences different? Do the texts present a Eurocentric point of view?

- If texts used are ethnocentric or discriminatory, highlight this as a point for discussion, and provide alternatives.

I go through a number of steps with the class to model to them how they can become critical readers. First, I choose a small number of short articles and read through these quickly with the class. I then demonstrate how to go through a number of processes, using the articles, such as:

  - *deciding the questions to be answered;*

  - *showing how to identify the main ideas and key points;*

  - *identifying topics of interest to look for within the text;*

  - *asking myself questions of the text to show my own thinking processes;*

  - *testing the validity of claims within the text;*

34

- *producing 'for' and 'against' arguments;*
- *adopting analytical approaches – showing how I would generally approach the text, as well as alternative strategies I might use;*
- *showing how to take notes sparingly from the text;*
- *demonstrating how to paraphrase and summarise and how to 'lift' without plagiarising.*

I then pose a small number of clearly worded questions that require them to give their opinion. We then discuss these and I try to show that I value their interpretations as well, that my interpretation can be questioned and that I sometimes find text problematic too. (Lecturer at an Australian university)

3.8 Working in groups

International students experience many difficulties with group work. This can mean that they miss the point of the educational opportunities that group work is intended to provide. They have difficulty joining in group work and report that they 'don't exist for home students' and don't get to experience the opportunities of working with British students that they had hoped for by studying in the UK.

International students can find group work difficult due to lack of language skills, lack of experience in this area, or lack of self-confidence, particularly when they have come from cultures where they have been expected to be self-effacing. Many international students feel that group assessments do not reflect their ability and believe that group tasks advantage home students. Many say they prefer individual assessments.

Working in groups with British students can sometimes make international students the target of criticism. Ledwith et al. (1998) found that: 'Students for whom English is their first language complain of having to rewrite the whole group assignment when the group is made up of students from a range of linguistic backgrounds.' They commented that this is perhaps an indication of lack of clarity about the role of English language in assessment. Students felt that their marks for individual work better reflected their ability than those given for group work. They found that home students preferred monocultural groups, whereas international students, particularly Asian students, preferred multicultural groups. They felt that this helped them to learn English as well as 'how we do things around here'.

Teachers need to recognise too how talking is used by different groups and can vary according to variables such as culture and gender. In Western cultures, it can be used to dominate a group or assert oneself. In Eastern cultures, it will tend to be used to create harmony and agreement within the group. In mixed groups, it is important to establish ground rules so that all students have the opportunity to contribute and so that the language and conventions (such as 'turn-taking') show respect for others and are not patronising, dismissive or excluding. Teachers must be prepared to question and challenge inappropriate language and address situations where students are being excluded.

Ledwith and Seymour (forthcoming) suggest that the time frame within which groups work impacts on their efficacy, with homogenous group working more effectively over shorter time frames, but diverse groups working increasingly effectively over time (catching up after around 17 weeks). They argue for task design specifically to incorporate training in intercultural skills for students:

> Intercultural competence, we suggest, is also related to time frame; and within Anglophone cultures working in time-present, a realistic period is needed to achieve high level performance … as models of behaviour and attitude change show, intercultural competence requires continuous reinforcement through training and development.

Teachers therefore need to plan group work with care.

As well as carefully planning the tasks that groups will undertake, teachers need to take a number of actions before, during and after group work tasks. They need to ensure that:

- groups are set up in ways that facilitate effective participation;
- interventions are planned that address potential or real problems that might arise within the group's processes and dynamics, and which facilitate more effective working within the group;
- assessment methods used are fair and do not disadvantage international students.

3.8.1 Setting group tasks

- Explain the rationale for group work.

If I don't engineer the composition of groups, then international students will tend to end up being in groups together. But I don't allocate groups until I have had a chance to get to know the students and have observed the dynamics of the whole group. If it is clear that some students or groups are likely to be left out or disadvantaged, then I allocate more vulnerable students to groups with more mature students in them.

(Lecturer, Oxford Brookes University)

- Especially for first-year students, set highly structured tasks initially and allocate set roles for each student.

- Provide a variety and choice of tasks and topics.

- Try to ensure that tasks are manageable and not over-burdensome.

- Break initial tasks into specific tasks for each group member so that everyone contributes early and ensures that everyone has a role.

- Try to allocate tasks and topics according to the interests or backgrounds of individuals within the group.

- In course handbooks, explicitly state that students will be required to work in multi-cultural settings and with students of different backgrounds, and will be required to work in groups and that they will be assessed as a group.

3.8.2 Setting up groups

- Mix the composition of the group but make sure that there is some homogeneity so that no individual feels isolated.

- If you know the students well, try to allocate international students to groups that may have better interactive skills, and ensure that there are a few international students in the group.

- Allocate students to diverse groups for some tasks and self-chosen groups for others.

- Provide training for all students or specific tasks on group formation and group working skills, and cross-cultural team working skills; include these as assessable learning outcomes.

- Have a pre-task ice-breaking exercise for the group to get to know one another, to make it easier for people to speak to others and the group, and so that students value each others' 'voices'

- Ensure that everyone understands the ground rules. These might include that:

  - the group will be diverse;
  - everyone is expected to participate;
  - others' contributions must be respected;

I used to think that it was best to spread the nationalities around – like one Malaysian in each group or if the British students were in the minority, one British student per group. Now I realise that they work better with some mutual support. So my rule now is if there are many students from one nationality, I pair them. Two or three international students in a group works best.

(Lecturer, Leeds University)

- everyone gets a turn;
- no-one should dominate or interrupt;
- everyone gets a turn at feedback to the whole group

3.8.3 Interventions during group work

- Observe interactions in groups or in group tasks – check that all students participate; observe body language or check comments in learning journals

- Briefly join the group and encourage more equal participation. If the problem persists, talk to the group explicitly about the problem

3.8.4 Fair assessment of group tasks

- Consider setting group work in order to pass the unit, but not including it in assessment

- Try to ensure that all students are able to reach higher levels of competency and achievement

- Recognise multiple perspectives and backgrounds and values

I was assessing the journal of an international student when I came to a passage where she had reflected on what was happening within her group. She described how she hadn't been getting along with a male British student who had at one point turned to her and said 'I'm going to "divorce" you.' 'I was so shocked', she wrote, 'In my culture divorce brings such shame. I cried all night.'

(Lecturer, Oxford Brookes University)

I have introduced an additional assessment component in group work to ensure that individual members' contributions are recognised.

I ask students to produce an individual 'reflective statement' on the process of working in a multicultural group, and ask them to report on:

- *the role they adopted within the group*
- *the working processes employed*
- *critical incidents*
- *the effectiveness of the group*

I also get groups to introduce 'functional pauses' during the group's work where one student acts as 'process leader' and is responsible for collecting views from all members of the group on the functioning of the group and its progress. This not only creates an environment where international students can participate more effectively but also offers the opportunity to group members to verify their acceptance of, and commitment to, the group's decisions.

(Lecturer, Oxford Brookes University)

- If using group work, it needs careful organisation to ensure that it:
  - includes skills development;
  - is long enough to develop effective relationships;
  - includes facilitation and intervention by staff;
  - assesses process and skills developed, not just output;
  - is at least partly carried out during taught sessions so that you can observe interactions and avoid placing a burden on students with heavy outside responsibilities.

Ask yourself

- Are groups the best method for completing given tasks?

- What are you assessing as outcomes of group work? (Process may be just as important as final outcomes. Criteria such as progress made by the group, or 'value-added' considerations could be assessed, or you could consider differential marking according to progress made by individual students.)

- Consider how long the group would take to complete the task, and whether the processes involved in making the group work would take time and effort away from its ultimate desired outcomes.

- Think about whether it would cause undue difficulties for particular groups of students, and whether it may cause inequalities of outcomes and rewards (especially when the task is a large percentage of marks). Could you use pair work instead?

3.9 Helping students to improve their study skills

Many international students will benefit from assistance in language and study skills. This will not only improve their ability to understand lectures and tutorials but will enhance their learning strategies,

We get the students in each group to do a number of tasks. The first one involves a short exercise evaluating a textbook, but before they get the book, they have to work on group formation processes such as how they are going to work together and allocate roles. We also ask them to establish the ground rules for the group. When they have completed these two tasks, they get a copy of the textbook to evaluate. At the end of the task, they are required to reflect on the processes of the group work, and provide suggestions of how they would improve these the next time.

(Lecturers, Oxford Brookes University)

improving their ability to demonstrate their knowledge in more sophisticated ways. Such classes can be offered prior to the student beginning their degree or while they are studying.

English language skills very often continue to be a challenge for international students and in some situations such as fast-paced lectures, some international students will be unable to process language correctly and at the rate necessary. Or they may be lacking in the particular language they need for their chosen discipline because their previous English language study may have been restricted to text books. Even when international students have achieved high TESOL scores, there may be little match between the English they have been trained to use and the way they need to express themselves in essays. They may also need assistance with library and computer skills.

> Language is at the heart of the matter for many international students and I believe that one should be very up front about this. I say to my students right at the start that they will be very frustrated because what goes down on paper will probably not reflect the quality of what is in their minds. We discuss this from the word go and I believe that helps. I also tell them that they will be assessed on the quality of what tutors perceive in terms of their thinking, not on the quality of their English per se, but that they have the challenge of making sure that the quality is perceivable. We do encourage preparatory English courses, even if the IELTS/TOEFL levels have been reached. We now have two strategies. One is to introduce ESP courses in advance which will not only help the student with their English in general, but will give them a fix on the technical/professional English they will need for the discipline. At the other extreme, we have a series of non-structured English classes in the School where there is an ELT teacher who will respond flexibly to the demands of the international student group week by week ('can we talk about how to operate in group work discussions' etc.). (Lecturer, School of Arts, Publishing and Music, Oxford Brookes University)

• • •

> Our University offers a Foundation Year for International Students which requires students to take three subjects, one of which is Undergraduate Study Skills in English. This is a large module which covers general learning skills such as using the library and computer skills and also provides training in assessment task methods such as how to give a presentation and how to structure

a seminar. The two other subjects are chosen from the student's planned area of study, such as maths and physics or chemistry for engineering students, maths and economics for business students and so on. Students attend mainstream lectures in these subjects, but special additional tutorials are held for international students. The Foundation Year covers transition issues as well as subject-specific issues including technical English and jargon used in subject areas. For example, Business students are required to study a 'Foundation Year English for Economic Studies' module. Opportunities are also provided for practical and laboratory work experience that the student may lack. We find that these opportunities for participating in practical tasks facilitates interaction between students and develops better relationships over time. (Leeds University)

3.9.1 Referring students for assistance

- Organise for students who may be having language problems to have a diagnostic language test if your university has an English language centre; even if the student has achieved high TESOL scores, this may have only tested a limited range of skills, so that they can still have difficulties with academic language and genres.

- Provide targeted study skills assistance or refer students to on-line learning skills programs mentioned above.

- Provide language and study skills assistance using the language and subject matter of the student's discipline. Language that is contextualised is more useful to students, and they can see the value of spending the extra time on it.

- Library induction courses should be provided to international students as a group so that the language used can be slower, and technical language and jargon can be explained. Students have more opportunities to ask questions.

3.9.2 Providing assistance within the school or faculty

- Provide as much study skills support at school or faculty level, ideally focusing on the tasks students have already been set, so that the activities used have the added benefit of providing learning within the discipline and counting towards their assessment.

Although all international students are tested for English language proficiency prior to admission, the University's Language Centre also tests all new international students whose first language is not English after they have registered with the University to identify students who may need extra language support during their course.

(Bradford University)

- Set early library and computer tasks, e.g. a survey of relevant journals in the discipline, a journal search for articles on a particular topic requiring students to use correct referencing, an Internet search, or a task requiring students to use software packages relevant to the discipline. More time can make all the difference.

- Do not be too quick however to refer students to outside language or study skills services, assuming that the student's language is the main problem. Make sure that you have first checked to ensure that it is not your own teaching practices that are causing problems for students.

We have been working with the University's International Centre for English Language Study, training groups of international students in study and sociocultural skills. We use the Excell Training Program (developed in Canada and Australia and recently piloted in the UK) which is designed to train students in the sociocultural skills they will need for academic success, such as: participation in a group or team setting; seeking help or information; making social contact and social conversation; refusing a request; expressing disagreement and giving feedback. Our participants have reported huge increases in their confidence and ability to interact successfully following the program.

(International Student Adviser, Oxford Brookes University)

It has been standard practice to refer students who are having difficulties with course work or assignments for language tuition or counseling. My position as Academic Learning Adviser for International Students included working with students, either individually or in groups, specifically targeting their perceived difficulties with the language of textbooks, or in completing assignments. In addition, skills training courses have been developed to assist with the induction of these students into the campuses. It was my role to initiate these courses for new students, focussing on what were assumed to be their projected needs. Many of these courses, and I would have to say this included the course(s) I was expected to teach, are based on outmoded unidirectional theories where the students is shown methods of time management, how to write essays and reports, and how to read academic texts, Again, these are premised on the notion that the student is the 'problem', whose needs are to be addressed and 'fixed up'. In general, little attention is given to exploring the teaching, learning and assessment practices which are occurring in the university classrooms, which may be impacting quite negatively on student learning. (Academic Learning Adviser for International Students at an Australian university)

- It may be useful however to provide international students with skills development training that assists them in developing generic skills that will be helpful to them right through their studies, such as assertiveness training and communication skills.

Assessment

4

Issues to do with assessment in relation to international students can be complex and frustrating for both sides. Students often feel disadvantaged by the methods used, and by their lack of background knowledge, implicitly assumed by lecturers to be in place. Teachers are concerned about maintaining standards and about practical implications, such as the amount of energy involved in doing things differently for international students. However, without some flexibility, these students will be disadvantaged and not receive fair treatment. As such there is a risk that assessment outcomes will not reflect their abilities. What is it, after all, that we are setting out to test? Whatever it is, there should be no question of 'lowering the standards' for international students or of 'going easy on them'. In the long run, this will not help them or you. Rather, it is a matter of finding ways that do justice to the talents and abilities of students who intrinsically do things differently. It is about finding alternatives that are just as rigorous as other methods, but that allow students to take different pathways in the demonstration of their capabilities and knowledge. It is also about removing any unnecessary or unfair barriers that students have no way of overcoming. It is about tailoring student assessment to student needs, within the requirements of the institution.

International students need assessment criteria that are clear, explicit and fair. Too often it is assumed that given tasks are easy to understand both in purpose and execution. International students will often not dare to ask for clarification. They need constructive feedback on tasks they have completed in order to improve. They need to be offered a range of assessment types that are flexible and negotiable and do the job that you want. The best tasks allow students to take advantage of their background knowledge and individual talents.

In their study of multicultural group work at Oxford Brookes University Ledwith et al. (1998) found that students from Asian countries were at the biggest disadvantage. Students not previously educated in the UK and especially those for whom English was not their first language, felt that their marks did not reflect their ability and were less comfortable with UK assessment methods, especially projects and investigations (both individual and group work), and seminar papers. These students were more likely to think that their English expression/grammar was being assessed, and were more likely than other students not to know if their fluency in English was being assessed. UK educated/English first language students had a clearer understanding of assessment criteria and were more aware of what they thought tutors expected to see – understanding of subject/topic, reading and research, analysis and interpretation, and use of academic sources. The researchers reported that this may be due to the students' difficulties in understanding the formal ways that assessment criteria are presented and reported that Asian students found tutor feedback on assessed work more helpful.

International students will also be generally unfamiliar with the marking systems of British universities, where marks tend to fall within a narrower band. Able students from American and Australian universities, for example, may be used to receiving marks in the 80s and 90s, and may be shocked when the first mark they receive is in the 60s. This needs to be explained very clearly to students before assessments are made, so that they understand that the rigour of assessment may be the same but marks mean different things in different systems, and so that they don't suffer loss of confidence.

4.1   Essays, assignments and presentations

It is not generally understood that many international students have little experience of writing essays or any other kind of written assignment. When they are required to produce written work, they may use a loose, unorganised style based on oral communication, which looks insufficiently planned.

In science areas, international students may be totally unfamiliar with the conventions of scientific writing, especially laboratory reports. They not only have to use advanced English language, but also be familiar with the layout, language and argument style appropriate to discipline-specific genres, and they need to learn how to do this in a very short time scale and with little support. There is a very big experiential gap between understanding what is required of them and how to comply with these new requirements.

4.2   Different writing styles

International students may also be unfamiliar with the styles of academic writing found in Western universities. A linear approach is generally taken in Western academic writing where the main theme is introduced first, and is followed by background information and supporting arguments. In other cultures a more circuitous approach may be taken where the reader is taken on a journey where the main point is only revealed at the end. Asian and African readers often see the Western preference for stating the main point first as bizarre and a 'give away'.

Carroll (1999) details how this happens:

> In the UK, people expect the key idea to be clearly expressed in the first, second or third line of the introductory paragraph of an essay. The 'good' student then spends the rest of the paper explaining, embellishing, arguing against or enriching the key point. This is a very different way from how, for example, a Nigerian might tackle the task. He might first spend considerable time making general, rhetorical points. He might offer personal beliefs and ask questions designed to acknowledge the reader's (or listener's) judgement and perspicacity. Then, when he felt he had given the reader a strong sense of the kind of person he (the writer) was and perhaps had won the reader to his side, he might begin to explore the issue – but still in a general way. It might be the middle of page two before the Nigerian writer makes any statement that a UK reader would recognise as germane to the argument. By then, the UK reader has probably given up, convinced the writer is disorganised. Rather than thinking 'Aha, he's using a different discourse style', the UK reader often thinks, 'He's waffling.'
>
> • • •
>
> Or an academic might be offered an essay written by someone from Hong Kong or Singapore where the thesis never gets stated at all. It's there – the student can assure the reader the thesis is there and point to how she offered sufficient cues to the reader to guess how the writer wished the argument to go. The student might argue that to just come out and state her views would be indescribably disrespectful to the reader. How could she, a student, imply that the reader, an experienced teacher, didn't know these things already? The reader is an expert – much better to show that the student/writer is aware of their common knowledge by hinting where the thesis lies. This approach shows respect because it means the writer trusts the reader to pay enough attention to his or her views to extricate them. Hong Kong students find the UK essay style astoundingly boring and banal. (Carroll, 1999)

45

Cortazzi and Jin (1997) describe how the essay style can pose difficulties for other international students:

> Some East European postgraduate students have difficulty understanding the British concept of an essay, particularly essay-type answers in exams. The reason is that, until recently, many Russians and East European university exams were oral. They involved students giving oral presentations on topics selected at random from a published list, which required extensive memorisation as preparation. The British tendency to dismiss this as 'rote-learning' could undermine these students' confidence in what they have been trained to do (successfully) in a particular culture of learning. The students' abilities in oral presentation could, of course, be harnessed in British seminar contexts and their ability to memorise need not be devalued, though complementary skills in analysis and critical evaluation will be required in the UK.

4.3 Different critical approaches

Critical approaches to the subject matter under discussion in an essay can be expressed differently by different cultures. Some approaches are more overt, others more subtle.

Quite often lecturers will criticise a student essay for not presenting an argument, or for losing the thread of an argument. Many international students will lack the language facility they need to construct a sophisticated argument in an essay.

> With a poor understanding of English usage it is difficult, although not impossible, to develop a highly intellectual and sophisticated argument. While the thought processes might be clear in the mind of the writer when thinking in the mother tongue, the transfer of these processes to vastly less sophisticated English often leads to a distortion of what was originally meant. Supervisors do not have the time to look for well-hidden lines of argument, and their assessment of the work will be influenced by the presence of poor surface structures. Poor English and poor argument or analysis can become inextricably linked. (Felix and Lawson, 1994)

4.4 Presentations

International students often lack the skills necessary for presentations, such as adequate language skills and self-confidence, as well as a lack of experience. In a stressful situation such as an oral presentation, international students can 'lose' their language skills, particularly if

The expression 'it is worthwhile to reconsider and discuss' was frequently used by Chinese writers to make an indirect criticism, as was the phrase 'some people have said', used without naming the people. In American academic writing, a different balance was found among various types of citations (background, supporting an argument, denoting criticism) in social science and science, indicating that writing happens in a particular way in different disciplines in American academic writing. It is not that some cultures are critical and others not, but that cultures express criticism in different ways.

Todd (1997)

they have had no previous experience of public speaking or if they come from cultures where they have been trained to be passive and self-effacing (see examples of alternatives to oral presentations in Chapter 3, section 3.7.2, p. 27).

International students therefore need explicit training in how to adapt to the styles of writing and presentation expected in their new environment.

4.5 Setting tasks

- Say things in the order that they are to be done .

- Provide a number of supplementary questions to the main essay question or topic that will give guidance as to what is required in their response.

- Ensure that essay 'prompts' can be easily deciphered, e.g. is the student expected to challenge the statement presented or to take a critical view of the topic?

- Set writing tasks in informal mode such as story-telling, letters, journals or dialogues where appropriate.

    I like to use Educational Portfolios to assess students' work. These allow me to see how the student's learning has progressed, to note a more confident use of English and discipline language, and to see examples of reflective learning which frequently capitalise on their experience of being international. Portfolios can contain a journal or learning log; review, report or essay; annotated bibliography; charts, posters, visual art; diagrams and graphs; examples of creative problem solving; video and audiotapes; computer discs; research and/or field notes. As portfolios call upon each student's ways of knowing, as well as their ability to explicate and demonstrate their knowledge using a variety of media, they are particularly valuable for international students as they can demonstrate their learning in ways that are not always text (language) based. The portfolios also allow students to develop an on-going relationship with the teacher, which builds on their language growth as well as their acculturation into the teaching and learning context of the University. (Lecturer, Australian Catholic University)

- Allow students to negotiate their own assessment tasks and topics, to take advantage of their educational skills and interests, and to negotiate their own learning outcomes.

- Allow international students to include background knowledge and experiences in assessment tasks, e.g. a contrast/comparison exercise using their own culture, or using a topic from their own culture as a basis for analysis using the concepts from the course. Some international students, however, will not see personal information as useful so this approach needs to be validated as appropriate to the topic. Sometimes international students are criticised for looking too locally and anecdotally, so they need help in how to express this kind of information in a way that is acceptable in an academic context.

4.6 Providing help to students

- Encourage students to use short, simple sentences.

- Encourage students to write an essay plan, using diagrams or concept maps to help them to realise that they need to organise their ideas prior to writing; explain that they may need to do a number of drafts.

- Provide examples of successful essays written by previous students, pointing out the range of different structures and strategies, and the flow of how an argument is established.

In my publishing course, I get students to consider the topic 'Finding ways to extend the market for children'. I ask students to reflect on their earliest reading experiences. Their task is to identify similarities and relate them to a proposed marketing strategies. Once I had a group with three students who came from Nairobi, Swindon and Buenos Aires. This group had had such a diversity of experiences, they came up with a whole range of different strategies.

(Lecturer, Oxford Brookes University)

- Choose simple topics to model with the class how essays addressing the topics can be structured. Model the first topic yourself, then ask the group to contribute ideas for the following topics, encouraging a range of alternative strategies and structures.

- Provide models of laboratory reports, pointing out the various parts and what must be included in each.

- Provide support to students when they are preparing presentations to enable them to develop the necessary skills, or consider alterations or alternatives that will make the situation less stressful.

4.7 Assessment and feedback

- Be prepared to assess work in progress, offering constructive criticism. To save time, focus on one issue such as structure, or assess the draft outline, or a part of the essay, and ask the student to work again on the essay, taking account of your comments.

- Allow students to negotiate weightings of assessment tasks according to the amount of effort required; for example, if a task takes an international student 50 hours to complete, compared with 30 for a home student, this could represent a higher percentage of their total mark.

- Address common problems with the whole class. Again this will save time, and will 'save face' for individual students; use real examples to demonstrate points.

- Check that your assessment methods and practices are fair. Do international students achieve as well as other students? Do they feel that their marks reflect their ability?

Ask yourself

- Do I expect all students to follow set formats and structures in essays and assignments?

- Do I value alternative writing styles?

- Do I provide assessment tasks that are flexible and can be negotiated to suit individual student's needs?

4.8 Exams

Many international students are seriously disadvantaged by exams, sometimes in ways it would be hard to anticipate. For example, Chinese students can be disadvantaged by multiple-choice questions as they view it improper to guess an answer. In addition, multiple-choice exams will often have phrases that are difficult to decipher, and may use double negatives. Although exams may be the most common method of assessment international students have previously experienced, the stress of examination conditions, particularly when they are time-limited, will have a deleterious effect on their performance. They will 'lose' their English, and will be restricted to using only what they are able to easily express in English. They may miss the subtle, and sometimes deliberately ambiguous, prompts in essay topics, which are designed to encourage students to adopt a challenging stance. International students may completely misunderstand these subtleties of language.

Obviously students who are working in a language that is not their own will have added difficulties when they have to use this language within the time limits of a test. Under such pressure they often find their languages get mixed up: some students report that they start thinking in a jumble of their own language and English. Others say they misread the wording of the instructions or questions in their panic, or they write down only those points they can express in English even when they know they are not really answering the questions.

(Ballard and Clanchy, 1997)

49

Short-answer tests are more like what many international students have previously been used to and may be more suitable for students to be able to demonstrate their abilities. It may be possible to offer students a choice, for example, one extended essay or three short-answer questions.

4.8.1 Exam topics and questions

• Use clear unambiguous language.

• Include a range of topics with ones specifically designed to allow international students to demonstrate their knowledge or perspective.

• Ensure that questions and subject matter can be understood by international students and are not Eurocentric.

• Use clear, straightforward English.

• Use short-answer exams.

• Consider allowing the use of dictionaries and providing extra time

• Some Australian universities allow non-English speaking background students, as well as students with some types of disabilities, to use dictionaries or laptops as well as having extra time, usually an additional 15 minutes per hour. Dictionaries and the hard drive on laptops are checked in advance to prevent cheating. This is not viewed as bestowing any advantage but rather to ensure that language does not act as a barrier to expression or comprehension.

4.9 Marking criteria

When you are assessing students' work, you need to be careful that the criteria you are assessing students against are consistent with the stated learning outcomes of the unit, and that you are not unconsciously marking down international students because of their lack of background knowledge or lack of English language facility. You need to think about whether you are unconsciously influenced by hidden agendas, such as personal bias about what you perceive to be academic ability.

In many types of assessment, international students can be seriously disadvantaged by their lack of background knowledge either of the subject matter or of more general information about the structures and

I asked the invigilator "What's a saucer?" in one multiple choice question. She said she couldn't tell me. But how would that have helped me with the answer? It was about English vocabulary, not international business decisions which is what the exam was about. I was so angry, I couldn't think well for the rest of the hour.

(Swedish student)

norms of the new culture. This may be particularly the case in areas such as Education, the Health Sciences or Social Work where personal experiences have helped to develop background knowledge. It can be extremely difficult for international students to make informed guesses or judgements about situations in a different culture.

More importantly, lack of English language facility can seriously disadvantage international students. Marking down for spelling or grammatical mistakes, where good spelling and grammar are not relevant or stated learning outcomes, can also lead to unfair assessments.

You may decide to ignore grammatical and spelling mistakes if meaning is clear. If the essay is difficult or impossible to read, the student should be given assistance to improve study skills, following which the essay can be re-marked. Staff in language centres or study skills advisers will sometimes provide advice to you about particular pieces of assessment.

> Universities need to provide not only linguistic support for overseas students but a subject-sensitive marking frame which acknowledges cultural as well as linguistic differences and does not make the error of assuming that concept and grammar can be simply unyoked. Merely refraining from deducting marks for poor grammar or spelling, for example, does not address the problem of the intellectual self-censorship of second language students: if one cannot express a complex idea, the idea will not appear. To address this reality – for example, by triangulating assessment methods – without lowering standards is a challenge for universities which wish to take both overseas students and academic rigour seriously; but to create within a competitive educational culture the acknowledgement that there is more than a single, traditional pathway to success may necessitate an institution-wide cultural shift. (Harris, 1995)

4.9.1 Assessment criteria

- Assessment criteria and tasks need to be explicit and clear, and explained verbally, with examples given wherever possible of your expectations.

- Make explicit any 'hidden agendas' in task setting or marking criteria such as if you deduct marks for spelling or if the style of presentation is considered important.

- If you assess for spelling and grammar, make sure that this is specified in learning outcomes and marking criteria.

In our School, we ask for two versions of the essay – one before it was edited, and then the edited version. This means that we can see the student's actual work, but also enables us to read it more easily.

(Lecturer, Oxford Brookes University)

4.9.2 Assessing sensitively

- Try correcting the student's English in the first few paragraphs and ask the student to correct the rest.

- Seek advice from staff from your university's English language centre or a study skills adviser (or refer the student for assistance).

- Recognise and reward different types of ability.

- Make sure that external examiners are aware of assessment policies and practices towards international students.

- Consider marking for 'value-adding', i.e. rather than expecting all students to meet a static level, consider assessing the level of progress made by individual students.

- Make sure that you explain the marking system in advance so that students are aware of what the grades of marks represent .

Ask yourself

- Do you assess for content or style?

- Do you unconsciously reward students for their 'cultural capital' – their facility with language and expression? Do you admire a confident and articulate style of argument? Do you reward students for essays that are easy to read? Do you unconsciously reward students for a style that is similar to your own?

- Have you examined the stated learning outcomes of the unit to ensure that students are being marked against these and not just your own personal prejudices or preferences?

4.10 **Feedback and criticism**

In many cultures, the teacher is seen more as a 'guru' and feedback can be seen as intensely personal. Feedback and criticism are extremely useful in encouraging international students to learn how to improve their learning, but it needs to be handled sensitively so that 'loss of face' can be avoided for students. Many international students will be intensely embarrassed by perceived failure, especially if they have not previously experienced this and have high expectations of themselves.

4.10.1 **Giving feedback**

- Try to give feedback in a positive, non-confronting way.

- Describe the behaviour, not the person, e.g. 'You set out the argument in paragraph one' not 'You are well organised and clear'.

- Give detailed, specific behavioural feedback with clear indications on how to improve.

- Try to show that you value student work, and that feedback is part of a learning process.

4.10.2 **Expressing criticism**

- Rather than giving feedback on an individual basis, do this anonymously with the whole group, highlighting common problems. This will be less time-consuming and will avoid students 'losing face'.

- Provide opportunities for structured, paired (mixed) peer feedback of written work.

- Many students will not be used to receiving criticism and will fear 'loss of face'. This can be avoided by the use of the 'third person', e.g. 'Sometimes people don't provide enough evidence to back up their arguments.'

- Be aware that a smile is sometimes used to hide embarrassment (both yours and theirs).

- Avoid using red ink.

4.11 Plagiarism and syndication

International students may have been previously rewarded for academic performance which drew heavily on the work of others. In some cultures this is regarded as a compliment to those whose work they copy (and is sometimes referred to as 'following the master'). In their new environment international students may find themselves being criticised and penalised for not being independent, or worse, being accused of plagiarism or cheating.

Such students may come from educational backgrounds where they were not required to present evidence of original thinking or to interpret knowledge. The concept of plagiarism may be entirely new to them and they are not aware that it is a requirement to acknowledge when they have borrowed from the ideas of others, and that not to do so is considered morally indefensible. Some may have trouble learning how to draw the line between quoting, embedding sources and plagiarism; they may not have the learning tools to get the balance right. They may need to put aside strongly held views such as believing that tampering with the written word is unacceptable. This is very hard to do. Also, international students often assume that teachers would know the sources and therefore do not consider it important to reference others' materials, and sometimes even believe that it would be offensive to teachers to imply that they were not aware of the material.

Denicolo and Pope (1999) make the point:

Our conventions, too, are derived from tradition and it is incumbent on us to make them explicit to others. A case in point is where we draw the line between authenticity and plagiarism, since for us acknowledgement of sources is an ethical issue while for others it is a latent assumption that all that we say is derived, in some way, from the work of others.

There has been much concern recently in Western universities about plagiarism and this has fallen hard on international students, especially those from collectivist societies, for whom such notions are often alien. Ballard and Clanchy (1997) point out,

> In a Confucian, Buddhist, Hindu or Islamic society, for example, the ability to quote from the sacred writings, from the sayings of the ages, from the words of leading scholars, is the essence of scholarship.

This tradition, however, also exists in Western societies, although now to a lesser extent. The ability to quote from great literary texts or poetry is still regarded as a sign of being well-educated and 'accomplished', although less so than in previous centuries.

The concepts behind the notion of plagiarism are culturally bound, with vast differences between Western societies with strong individualistic ideologies, and collectivist societies. The concept of individual ownership of ideas runs contrary to the ideas of collective ownership in these societies. Scollon (1995) argues that perhaps some students cannot understand the notion of plagiarism due to their cultural heritage:

> The apparent difficulty that at least some non-native writers of English have in correctly using reference, quotation, and paraphrase, and in avoiding plagiarism, might be better construed as reflecting a different ideological base. That is, some of this difficulty should be understood not as an inability to learn something simple, but rather as unconscious resistance to an implicit ideology of what has been called 'the potent private self' (Moerman, 1988: 67). (Scollon, 1995)

It is not enough merely to tell students that they must not plagiarise and to provide them with a simple definition of plagiarism. International students need to be shown what they should be doing. They need training in how to paraphrase, how to synthesise information from a wide range of sources, how to 'mine' text for suitable quotes, and how to weave sources and quotes into their own work. These are very sophisticated techniques that require a high level of language facility. Home students may equally borrow their information from the work of others, but may simply be more adept at using different words and phrases to disguise the product to appear as their own.

Similarly, collusion, or syndication, is not considered wrong in many collectivist cultures but is seen as cooperation among the group. Resources are expected to be shared among the group, including ideas and opinions.

I give students simple descriptions of plagiarism and collusion:

- *Copying – reproducing or imitating*

- *Collaboration – working with others*

- *Collusion – agreement to deceive; using the words or ideas of colleagues or other students and passing them off as your own*

- *Plagiarism – stealing someone's words or ideas and passing them off as your own*

I then give the students real examples of each of these.

(Lecturer, University of Strathclyde)

I was given no advice or guidance about the format and layout of a project this size and was certainly not told about the need for footnotes or how to refer to source materials used...I am trying to argue it could not have been plagiarism because I did not intend it and I referenced the book as I had always done.

(Student charged with plagiarism who won the appeal)

4.11.1   Giving advice on how not to plagiarise

- Discuss what is meant by plagiarism and give real examples.

- Explain the difference between paraphrasing and plagiarism.

- Demonstrate to students how to paraphrase, synthesise and weave other sources into their own work.

- Show how to meet referencing requirements and why they are required.

- State where syndication is not permitted, describing what this means and why it is unacceptable

- Explicitly state the consequences of not complying with rules against plagiarism and syndication

I begin by discussing with the students why we need a good range of vocabulary when paraphrasing. We then discuss what kinds of things we should always keep and not substitute, so that plagiarism is avoided. I then get the students to write down in their own words a definition for plagiarism, and then a definition for syndication. Definitions are then compared, and on an OHP, with feedback from me, we produce a satisfactory negotiated definition of these terms.

During the session, the students have 8 questions to consider in guiding this work:

- *What do you understand by the term plagiarism?*

- *What do you understand by the term syndication?*

- *If you want to copy the exact words from another writer into your writing, how do you avoid plagiarism?*

- *If you change the words you have read, by paraphrasing the ideas of another writer, how do you avoid plagiarism?*

- *How much should you use acknowledged quotations from other writers in your writing?*

- *What else do you need to do in your writing if you are going to introduce the ideas of another writer through paraphrase?*

- *Why is it very important to make an accurate bibliography in your writing?*

- *How can you let the writer know, directly or indirectly, whether you agree or not with another writer's ideas when you quote them?*

(Lecturer, Oxford Brookes University)

Course content and design

5

The previous chapters have looked at how individual teachers can take action to improve their individual teaching and learning practices. But course content and design are equally important. Consideration needs to be given to designing into the curriculum and course content good teaching practices for international students.

Lecturers need to 'step back' to see that course content and design are as culturally embedded as teaching and learning processes. Some commentators have questioned, for example, the wisdom of slotting international students into courses that have been designed for so-called 'first world' students, who will predominantly be working in Western environments following their studies. The 'world view' presented in these courses may provide no connections for international students and may be of little value to them in their future careers. Business studies courses, for example, may be concerned with talking about industrialised economies which may have little relevance for other countries.

Learning theories commonly state that students construct meaning by relating new information to previous knowledge and personal experience, by 'hooking' into the student's existing schemata. Unless international students are able to use their background knowledge and learn how to apply it to new situations, they will have difficulty building new knowledge. It is therefore important that course content covers a broad range of perspectives so that the learning experiences of all students can be built on and enhanced. The historical, cultural, political, socio-economic perspectives from which subjects are viewed are determined by the choices made by staff about content and design of courses.

Ames (1996) argues that internationalising the curriculum will also lead to better integration of international and home students.

> It is clear from recent research, that one of the main reasons why international students choose to study outside their home country is to experience living and studying in a different culture, and yet

the experience of many international students studying in the UK is that they find it difficult to integrate with UK students. A curriculum which provides the opportunity for students to consider the international dimensions of their subjects is likely to provide a far more fertile ground for collaboration between staff and students across cultural divides, and to do so in a way which values the contribution of, and is of value to, all participants.

5.1 Course content

Many international students complain that their courses offer an almost exclusively anglocentric view in some areas of study, and that this view is presented as if it were universal. Even when students raise the point that what they are being taught will be of limited value to them when they return to their own culture, this point is often ignored.

Often, lecturers find it hard to imagine how they could incorporate an international dimension into what they teach. They often say things like 'I teach Chemistry. Where's the international dimension in that?' But in the examples they use, and in teaching ways of applying knowledge in different situations, they can give a diversity of examples and use a variety of methods. Alternative cultural ways of viewing a discipline can be important in understanding why a discipline has evolved in a particular way in different cultures. For example, we can look at why Western science has evolved in the way that it has, and what alternative approaches exist, or why different cultures use different mathematical counting systems such as using ten as a base or even three or five.

I tried to explain to the lecturer that only learning about British secondary schools wasn't of much use to me, that I needed to look at broader principles and how I could apply them back home. He told me that I should learn from the British educational system because then I could show people in my own country how schools should be run. The emphasis in the unit had been on the importance of using information and communication technology in the classroom. In my part of Kenya, schools don't have any computers!

(Masters student from Kenya)

Ask yourself

- Examine your own discipline. Are you aware of its cultural heritage? Do you know if it has been predominantly constructed by a particular culture/period in time/personalities/schools of thought?

- Has this been to the exclusion of other schools of thought or influences? Do you try to include alternative viewpoints or ones that are critical of the conventional approaches?

- Do you use materials that contain a range of social, political, economic and religious perspectives, events, theories and achievements?

5.1.1 Include international perspectives

- Try to include an 'international dimension' in the course and course materials, which reflects the increasing globalisation and internationalisation of the discipline.

- Use the curriculum to alert home students to global and international perspectives, to prompt them to discover alternative perspectives and paradigms, and to develop cross-cultural awareness and skills.

- Consider broadening the choice of units within the course to provide units that give an international perspective to your discipline, e.g. marketing in Asia; international human resources management; architecture in different cultures; health care practices in other cultures; town planning in poor, hot countries or countries with little infrastructure.

5.1.2 Being inclusive

- Ensure diversity of images, examples, case studies, and texts in course materials used.

- Include content from other cultures, perspectives and philosophies.

- Try to establish a common base of knowledge in the discipline such as covering legislative frameworks or government policies, historical events or influences, key identities, organisations or concepts, and useful journals and references.

5.1.3 Establish international collaborations

- Strengthen the international content and perspective of courses through specific projects with overseas universities, and try to provide opportunities for students (both home and international students) to work within these projects during their studies.

- Encourage the establishment of research collaborations between individual members of staff and staff at overseas universities to broaden the subject area and perspectives of those members of staff.

5.1.4 Use international expertise

- Invite outside experts with international knowledge or from overseas countries to present lectures or seminars giving international perspectives and examples.

- Explain where appropriate that issues such as race and gender will be covered in the course and that the language used to describe such issues can be value-laden and even offensive to other cultures.

- Positively celebrate diversity and internationalisation.

An exercise we use in the MSc in International Hotel and Tourism entails students contributing information from their own region to relate it to the theories and themes of the course. Students are predominantly from overseas. Students are divided into groups according to the geographic region from which they come. They are then given the following tasks:

1. *Discuss the main things that have been happening in your region of the world over the last ten years in the following two areas:*

   - ***Social trends** (e.g. demographic changes, role of women and the family, levels of education, feelings/beliefs about involvement in decision-making at different levels of society, social problems ...)*

   - ***Economic trends** (e.g. growth/recession, share of world markets, relative wealth/poverty, employment/unemployment importance of service industries and tourism in particular, income distribution, taxation...)*

2. *Record on the paper provided 3 key social trends and write down the impact these trends have on:*

   - *the hotel industry in your region*
   - *approaches to managing people in your region*

Students then report their findings to the group. This exercise provides the students not only with an opportunity to contribute their own knowledge and experience, but they also become resources for the whole class and in one session, the entire group receives a global picture of the current relevant issues in the industry. (Lecturers, Oxford Brookes University)

5.1.5 Use international students and staff as resources

- Design courses to require the sharing of experiences and cultural expertise.

- Use international students as a resource in identifying more international perspectives and materials.

- Identify other teaching staff with international experience who would be willing to share their knowledge and lend support.

- Use your international students as 'living resources' – consult with them about the selection of appropriate course materials and design.

I teach a unit for English teachers where I work with students to identify the topics to be covered each year. Most students are from overseas, and all are experienced teachers of English, with a wide variety of backgrounds. I give students a long list of topics that could be covered, and then students work together to identify those most relevant and useful to them. Each student first prioritises topics according to their individual needs, and then in groups of four, students produce a prioritised list for their group. During this phase, students are encouraged to talk to each other about their backgrounds and their needs. The small groups then report to the whole group, with a student chairing the discussion, and the class comes up with a joint list. This helps students to have some responsibility for the unit but also helps to validate its content in light of the past experiences and future needs of the students.

I also use students themselves as resources such as when working on the design of English tests. We look at examples from a variety of education systems, using what the students consider to be 'good' and 'bad' examples, and students use these to develop general principles. They then critique their own system's methods and use the general principles developed to design tests that would be suitable for that system, challenging them to reconsider, but not dismiss, the validity of different approaches in different contexts. (Lecturer, Leeds University)

5.2 Course materials

- Ensure that course materials such as unit guides and handbooks are available that use clear language to explain the key concepts and ideas within the course. Students need clear access to meaning, to be able to develop common understandings of the keys concepts and ideas of the course and to fill in the gaps in their background knowledge. Many international students may come from areas with vastly different economic, political and social systems and the various terms and concepts used may have different uses and meanings.

- Provide all course materials in simple English.

- Give clear descriptions of course learning objectives including specific expectations of the skills students are expected to develop such as: working independently, thinking critically, using a number of sources, actively participating in class activities, working independently in the library, expressing personal opinions, allowing others to participate in group discussions, learning to respect and value the opinions and backgrounds of others.

- Provide a glossary of commonly used terms, acronyms and abbreviations (make sure that your explanations assume no background knowledge).

We have developed a series of Study Guides for courses that are taught overseas as well as in the UK, to ensure that students have access to common information and materials. These give detailed information on the key topics, ideas and concepts of the course. For each section of the course, we give specific information on the desired learning outcomes, resources available (including texts), detailed descriptions of the major issues and topics within each section, and bibliographies. For example, the International Business course study guide defines economic terms and concepts in international trade and describes major institutions such as the World Bank, the International Monetary Fund, and the World Trade Organisation. This ensures that students develop understandings of the international bodies and global forces beyond their own borders. The Study Guides were written by Petja Tanova from the University of National and World Economics in Sofia, Bulgaria, where some of our courses are offered, as we wanted to widen our own academic base and include culturally different perspectives to enrich the course for international students. (The University of Lincolnshire and Humberside)

Ask yourself

Do an 'audit' of your course materials and design and ask yourself:

- are they accessible and understandable for international students?

- will they meet the educational needs of international students?

- will they make sense to international students?

- will international students be able to identify with and make sense of the examples and case histories used?

- will international students be able to use their own experiences and backgrounds?

5.3 Course texts

- Provide a list of texts and readings that is prioritised and annotated.

- Ensure that these texts are suitable for beginning students.

- Work with library resource staff to identify internationalised textbooks and international materials, case studies and examples within your discipline.

- If texts used in the course are culturally offensive, stereotyping, ethnocentric or narrow in perspective, provide other texts to balance this or specifically point out the biases in the text.

5.4 Course evaluation

Very little evaluation is carried out by universities in the UK on whether their courses fulfil the expectations of international students. Do you know whether international students have pass and completion rates comparable with home students? Pass and completion rates tend to be higher for courses that are specifically designed for international students, but considerably lower for students in mainstream courses. Are international students then getting good value for money? How much support, academic and social, is provided to them? The UK spends considerably less on support services for international students than, for example, the US or Australia.

Universities need to look more carefully at whether courses are meeting the needs of international students and whether they are achieving good outcomes and completion rates in their chosen fields of study.

- In course evaluations, make sure that you include issues of relevance to international students, such as asking if students felt disadvantaged by the assessment methods used, whether background information was assumed, or if students were able to use their own experiences and beliefs in course activities and assessment tasks.

- Use both formal and informal evaluation methods such as discussions or interviews with individual students as well as questionnaires, both during and at the end of the course.

- Ask students if their broader needs, not just academic needs, were met.

- Include evaluations of student outcomes to check if international students are obtaining the same success and completion rates as home students.

- Include pre-arrival surveys as well so that you are aware in advance of students' needs and expectations.

We recognise that it is important to evaluate whether we are adequately catering for the needs of overseas students. We have in place institutional mechanisms that do this such as through regular module and programme evaluation by anonymous questionnaire.

(University of Newcastle)

Issues for personal tutors

6

In addition to the teaching, learning and assessment issues outlined above, teachers who have a responsibility for the broader welfare of international students need to be sensitive to the particular pressures that can impact on international students. In the personal tutor, international students may find the role and relationship that they are more accustomed to having with teachers in their home culture. Tutors may sometimes find that international students can be demanding of their time so it is important to explain your responsibilities and the boundaries of the relationship early. Make sure that you let students know when you will be available and when you will not be available. Your role will be an important one in easing the transition of students and supporting them to successfully complete their studies. They may need assistance in building up their skills, their confidence and their support networks. You also need to be sensitive to the pressures on international students to succeed and the importance of referring students to support services early before real problems set in.

6.1 Names

Make sure that you know international students' names, what students like to be called, and check with them that your pronunciation is correct. Let students know how you wish to be addressed and encourage them to learn other students' names.

Ask for someone's first name, rather than Christian name. Many Chinese names have the family name first followed by the 'personal' name or names so it may be better to ask for their full name and then what they wish to be called. Sometimes students, especially Asian and African students, will adopt a western name when they are overseas if they perceive that their own name will be difficult for foreigners to pronounce. Students often appreciate however when teachers make the effort to find out if students prefer their own name to be used, and make sure that they pronounce it correctly. Many international students will feel uncomfortable calling their teachers by their first name if this is not done in their own cultures, and it is only a relatively recent practice in Western universities.

6.2 Fear of failure

Motivations of international students may be very different from those of home students. In Confucian heritage societies, respect for elders and the concept of 'face' have major influences on motivations for study and even what students choose to study. Failure is seen as a result of not working hard enough, leads to loss of face, and for students returning, may result in isolation, strong disapproval and sanction from the family. Also, many international students will have only been able to study overseas through heavy borrowings from family and friends and they may be expected to contribute to the education of siblings upon return. Failure therefore can have serious consequences for international students. Fear of failure will also undermine confidence and can encourage the use of superficial approaches to learning.

6.3 Early contact

• Make the first move, as many international students find it hard to approach their tutor without an explicit invitation. Make sure you require some kind of an initial contact to ensure that they don't lose face by having to approach you when they have a problem.

• Make sure you get the student's name right so that you are comfortable using it.

• Provide structured guidance, especially when the student is new.

• Encourage students to increase the amount of initiative they take themselves.

• Invest time at the beginning to avoid later problems.

6.4   Providing support

- Make it clear that you are approachable. Let students know how and when they can see you and make sure that you allocate enough time to them.

- Try to provide a non-judgmental, sympathetic listening ear.

- Try to be empathetic: see the problem from the student's point of view.

- Make it clear that it is common for students to experience problems and that it is legitimate for them to seek your help.

- Try to assist students to build up their own support networks such as through student associations and clubs, student social activities, pairing or peer mentoring programmes, activities in their courses, or by joining outside community groups.

In the Examination Unit we are piloting a scheme – 'Directed support measures for International Students experiencing academic difficulty' – where we are working with personal tutors to try to improve the retention levels of international students as we had identified that a significant number are required to re-sit examinations each year.

The scheme involves identifying a group of international students at the beginning of Term 1 who may be at risk of failure. Personal tutors, using a pro-forma set of questions, work with the student to identify possible underlying risk factors and potential causes of failure. For non-academic factors, the student is referred to other specialist support services in the University.

If academic factors are identified, an Individual Academic Action Plan (IAAP) is developed which identifies the learning strategies the student is responsible for working on, and the particular support arrangements that will be provided to them. Meetings are held with the student in Terms 1 and 2 to review goals and strategies, and in Term 3 the student and tutor meet to review the student's progress, and put in place any extra strategies for the rest of the term to improve the student's performance. So far, the group of students involved has had fewer failures than a control group. (Examination and Conferment Unit, Oxford Brookes University)

6.5 **Boundaries and referral**

- Set boundaries and limits that you are comfortable with. Let the student know what you can and can't do, and who else is available to help.

- Refer students to specialist support services when you no longer feel comfortable or competent to deal with a student's problem.

- Seek advice from specialist support services if you are unsure whether to refer on, or wish to explore options for responding to a student's problem.

Postgraduate supervision

7

7.1 Relationship and boundaries

In the same way as for undergraduate international students, international postgraduate students will be shaped by their previous educational experiences and expectations. They are likely to expect a hierarchical relationship with their supervisor where the supervisor exercises tight control over the research. Many international students will expect their supervisor to take the initiative and adopt a role close to being a guide and/or parent. They may expect their supervisor to make major contributions towards the research and the thesis. They will be expecting clear direction and guidance from their supervisors, whom they will hold in great esteem, and they will often have very high expectations of the relationship. They usually assume the supervisor to be very knowledgeable in their area of study.

Many will be totally unprepared for the independence and isolation of postgraduate study. They may be unfamiliar with the extending and speculative approach expected of postgraduate students and the expectations of the creation of 'new knowledge' may be culturally foreign for them. They may have no experience of literature searching, critical reading, or specialised research skills. They may be lacking in library, computer and laboratory skills. Of course, home students may feel the same sense of surprise and disappointment but may have many more skills and strategies for adapting and negotiating a suitable relationship with supervisors.

On taught courses, international students complain of too little structure and too little control exercised by staff. On research-only courses, international students will often only have their supervisor to relate to, and the relationship therefore becomes paramount. The first six months are crucial, and this is the time when the relationship needs to be clearly negotiated and understood.

The relationship between student and supervisor will be further complicated by the fact that there are no explicit rules for supervision of postgraduate students. These are often developed as a result of the supervisor's own experience of supervision, information derived from broad guidelines produced by the institution, or may be simply based on tradition. For students who have come from education systems where teacher–student relationships are hierarchical and clearly defined, international postgraduates may be bewildered by the lack of clarity in their new relationship with their supervisor and some may seek to establish relationships closer to what they were expecting to find.

7.2 **The supervisor's view**

The relationship can be a difficult one for supervisors as well. Supervisors report that international students require a considerable amount of their time and energy and that a lot of this time is taken filling in gaps in their background knowledge, and in their practical experiences.

Ryan and Zuber-Skerritt (1999) state:

[concerns of supervisors] range from possibly inadequate language skills in English, culturally-based conceptualizations of knowledge and consequent learning styles, inculcation into the disciplinary discourse and poor disciplinary preparation (Felix and Lawson 1994), to differing expectations of the roles of student and supervisor. There is for many supervisors the additional complication of a lack of understanding of the many varied cultures from which their students derive, and the effect of these on the students–supervisor relationship.

Many international students feel that it is important that their supervisors have some knowledge of their home country and understanding of their culture. The importance of an empathetic relationship between student and supervisor is illustrated by the story of a Chinese postgraduate student in Australia, quoted in Ryan and Zuber-Skerritt (1999). The student explained her experiences in finding a new, sympathetic supervisor after having a poor experience with an unsympathetic one:

> He taught me how to adjust my thinking to accommodate Western ways – together we built a bridge that I could cross … Everything I said, he understood … I laugh – he laughed. He very much understands the ways of the Chinese student. He went to teach in China and he understands the Chinese culture and educational system. He is able to understand the Chinese students and the difficulties we face here. He also understands why I have come here … He would ask me what it was that I was thinking about in my writing. I would just know the main ideas and he would help me find the hidden meanings in the books that I am reading. One paragraph at a time he would explain things and show me the argument that he would make. I soon learned that making this argument was not easy but as I changed my ways, I could do it too. He showed me how to do this. He knew that I was not stupid because he understood the Chinese ways. I have never thought this way before and I am learning that it is a good way to think. At the moment I am not perfect but I am getting better.

7.3 **Problems in the relationship**

Postgraduate international students can experience enormous difficulties, particularly if there are misunderstandings with their supervisor. They can start to withdraw and become very isolated, and some go into a downward spiral. They then need a 'lifeline' of some kind to bring them back on track. One international student retreated into the postgraduate study room, and began virtually living there. He was eventually befriended by a cleaner, who gave him items he needed to survive, and this was the only thing that prevented him from giving up his studies and returning home. Another became completely isolated in his Faculty, to the point where he had contact with no-one and the staff were completely unaware of the work he was doing in the laboratory. He complained of racial discrimination by other members of staff and was ostracised. Eventually another member of the teaching staff befriended him, asked about his background and his country, and took an interest in his work. It became clear that there had been a misunderstanding between him and his supervisor that had lead to the situation arising. After this, he was able to continue his work successfully.

If you allocate supervisors:

- try to ensure a good and productive match of student and supervisor, where there is mutual knowledge and respect;
- try to allocate supervisors with overseas experience, intercultural sensitivity or intercultural communication skills, strong empathetic skills, or who have background knowledge of the student's home country or culture.

If you are a supervisor:

- clarify roles of both student and supervisor early;
- discuss expectations of both sides to avoid future misunderstandings;
- set boundaries and limits to what you are prepared to do;
- schedule regular appointments which both parties are responsible for keeping;
- record decisions made during meetings;
- provide more assistance early and gradually assist the student to develop more independent learning approaches;

- try to assess where your student is academically and their knowledge of the discipline;
- do not assume background knowledge in the subject area.

7.4 **Recognise added pressures**

- Be sensitive to the fact that international students may be undergoing enormous cultural change and stress.

- Recognise that it will be difficult for some students to express dissatisfaction or criticism. Try to 'read between the lines'.

- Recognise that they have to work a lot harder than other students, especially in the time taken to do background reading.

- Be aware of different ways of expressing needs and difficulties.

7.5 **Provide practical advice**

- Try to assist students to identify key texts and authors so that they don't waste valuable reading time on texts that are not useful.

- Provide advice on general texts that will fill in gaps in background knowledge.

- Identify a small number of key texts or articles for the student to read at the beginning of their studies.

- Assist the student to identify the key current debates within their area of study.

- Regularly check that the student is making progress.

- Alert students to conferences being held in their area of study, or other scholars with whom they should make contact.

- Try to facilitate their contact with other students for learning and social support.

At the interview, I was trying to give a good impression to the admission officer with how I would normally behave in front of a person of authority in Japan – that is, 'Be polite, say little and accept authority.' I apologized to him for my poor language skills. His decision was that I should attend classes on campus for a term to improve my English before starting the coursework. After a month or so, I found that the classes were not helping me at all. They were for general-purpose English and had no focus. I felt I was wasting my time. I thought I needed to improve my language in the academic context and went to discuss this with the same admission officer. I was more assertive than the previous time. He said, 'You speak English all right. If you had spoken like you are now when you arrived, I would have accepted you in the program straight away.' This incident made me realize that my approach to authority might work in my own cultural environment, but had worked against me in the American system. It was true culture shock. (Nagata, 1999)

7.6 Improving research skills

A common problem is that supervisors assume too much of students' research knowledge. But some international students will have very little knowledge on how to conduct research. They need considerable guidance in the early stages of their research in their specific research area, as well as in a range of skills such as advanced research methods, computer and literacy skills, and assistance in how to find sources and materials. They may also be severely lacking in necessary background knowledge in the discipline. They not only need to improve their general research skills but also need to be gradually introduced to the academic discourse of the discipline so that they can start to become active members.

You may find that your international students are severely lacking in practical experiences and this needs to be investigated. In the sciences, they may be lacking in laboratory experience and may need assistance with laboratory practices and protocols. They may have previously learnt in a paper-orientated way, rather than through activity-based learning. International students with little laboratory experience, or who have worked in laboratories that are less well equipped, or had less technically advanced equipment, may need more training and assistance from demonstrators and technicians. They may also need more help with reading technical instructions and manuals. Working on practical tasks in small groups in the laboratory with other students can be an excellent tool for international students in facilitating interaction and improving their language and communication skills.

Similarly, some international students may have fewer, or less advanced, computer skills, and will need extra assistance. They will need clear instructions, and information needs to be given in small

An example that comes to mind is a postgraduate student who began his dissertation with a poetic description of an event far removed in focus from his main thesis topic. To his supervisors this introduction seemed at best irrelevant, and he had initial difficulty in being taken seriously. In fact, within his culture, one never begins with the main point. But his supervisors saw him as rambling or beating about the bush. They did not see that he might be writing to a different but equally valid agenda. When this was clarified, they were able to enter into his work and see it as very original and good. The problem for students like this is that they are not given any hard and fast official ruling on how to present ideas. It is vital for the lecturer as reader /audience/ supporter to give appropriate and constructive guidance, to help students adapt to the expected but implicit 'norms' of academic culture.

(Errey, 1994)

'chunks' with opportunities for practice. They will need to have their new learning reinforced by frequent practising of their new computer skills. Some international students of course will come from educational systems that have more access to information and communications technology, such as students from the US and Singapore.

7.7 Organise training in special skills

• Arrange for international postgraduates to receive training in basic laboratory skills and protocols.

• Place undergraduate international students in laboratory groups with home students who already have good laboratory skills and knowledge.

• Where safety in a laboratory exercise is paramount, ensure that instructions have been understood by asking students to do a 'dry run' of the procedures required first, before using the actual equipment.

• Provide guidance on how to obtain background knowledge, research skills, computer skills, and critical literacy skills. Many universities provide targeted programmes for international postgraduates in these areas.

7.8 Writing

Many international postgraduate students will have had very little experience in any kind of extended writing, and may have previously only been required to take lecture notes (see also Different writing styles, Chapter 4, section 4.2, above). They may therefore resort to an oral style, or may use writing styles that are favoured in their own country.

The use of proverbs, stories and literary allusions, for example, are commonly used in Asian and African writing to demonstrate one's educational level and accomplishment, to win the reader over to the author's point of view and to establish credibility. Classical sayings or poetic phrases will be used to make the writing look 'well-educated' and to establish empathy. The writing process takes a more circuitous approach, where the reader is gradually taken along a journey where the argument, or main thesis, is only found at the very end. The thesis will begin by describing what the topic isn't before writing about what it is.

The ICELS (International Centre for English Language Studies) at Oxford Brookes University offers not only foundation courses in language and study skills, but also provides a thesis-checking service for international postgraduate students. Other universities sometimes employ an editor or reviewer to examine first drafts of theses. Some universities allow thesis drafts to be written in the student's first language and are then translated.

- Ask for written work early and discuss content and layout, but avoid editing or rewriting work at this stage.

- Encourage international postgraduates to look at previous theses and use them to discuss different approaches and structures used; ask them to discuss these theses critically.

- Encourage them to keep a learning journal and compile a glossary of new words, terms and concepts.

- Show how to use sources without plagiarising, demonstrating how to paraphrase and synthesise.

Experiences of international students and what universities can do to help

8

8.1 Culture shock and adjustment problems

Although the majority of international students successfully complete their overseas studies, they can experience severe difficulties, especially in the initial period of their study. University study is inherently stressful, but international students can experience a range of additional difficulties. They are no longer in familiar surroundings, and are away from the support structures provided by family, friends and their community. They may be financially independent for the first time or they may be suffering a significant loss of status from their former position. They are at higher risk of academic failure and of dropping out. The enormous pressure to succeed puts further pressure on them; they will feel the fear of failure acutely and may feel embarrassed when they don't get the marks they have been used to.

> The experience of studying in a foreign country leaves a powerful impression on young people that may last all their lives ... For some young people it is the most important experience of their lives and one that turns them into loyal advocates of the country they study in ... In an increasingly international world they can be fine ambassadors of good international relations. Yet they remain vulnerable to the debilitating effects of culture shock which educational authorities would do well to be sensitive to, and be ready to treat accordingly. (Furnham, 1997)

Many writers describe the experiences of international students as a cycle, from honeymoon period, to a stage of depression, rejection, hostility and withdrawal, then finally adjustment, autonomy and independence, then a readjustment period after returning home.

The greater the cultural shift in terms of language, values, customs, philosophies and ideology, as well as other factors such as diet, climate and geography, the more the student is likely to experience difficulties and distress. International students report a higher incidence of medical conditions and mental health problems, and even feelings of grief, but they are less likely to use counselling services, possibly because they perceive them to offer Western attitudes and solutions. They are more likely to use cultural friendship groups for support.

Friendship networks are extremely important in helping international students to cope with the demands of living in a new culture and in surviving in the new academic environment. Furnham and Bochner (1986) identified three types of friendship networks that are important for international students. Monocultural groups comprising other international students provide support for coping with loneliness, homesickness and adjustment problems; bicultural networks with home students provide advice on how to navigate the university and outside environments; and multicultural networks provide companionship for recreational and non-academic activities. International students need all three types of networks if they are to be successful in their studies.

8.2 Impacts on cognition

The initial period of study is the most difficult time for international students. Culture shock can produce a number of negative side-effects and students can experience overwhelming physical symptoms from stress-related disorders. They may feel overwhelmed and over-react to situations, may become overly dependent on co-nationals, feel anger and resentment towards those from the host country and may have difficulty with ordered, sequential thinking resulting in their making illogical or precipitate decisions such as wanting to change courses, drop out or return home. They may experience a range of problems with their study such as procrastination with assessment tasks and experience a range of impacts on learning.

The stresses involved in studying overseas can have a range of impacts on cognitive functioning, such as :

- thinking (including concentration, focus, memory, critical thinking);
- behaviour (motivation, fluctuating energy levels, apathy, isolation, alienation);
- affects (anxiety, panic, confusion, frustration, anger, disorientation, depression, insomnia, paranoia);
- judgement and insight (psychosocial and self-reflective skills deficits which hinder ability to seek assistance or make optimal decisions).

8.3   Loss of identity and self-esteem

There can be significant effects on self-esteem and confidence for many international students, and loss of status and identity.

When students are unable to express themselves properly, or in as complex or sophisticated manner as they would like, they begin to lose confidence and self-esteem. They start to feel like a non-person, stripped of all of their usual resources for coping and expressing themselves. They can feel like they are becoming a different person.

> I have had to accept many things I do not approve of and it is such a shock to me because of my own customs. It is as though everything I have been taught at home and all my values do not count for anything here and I must become a different person to cope with it all. I think if my family could see me now they would think I had changed very much, to accept such things that are completely against my upbringing. (student quoted in Harris, 1995)

8.4   How the university can help: the broader environment

8.4.1   Getting the welcome right

If you have a broader role within your department or school, there are a number of things that you can do at this level to improve the chances of success for international students.

The first arrival period for international students is crucial in determining their future chances for success. Studies of non-completion of students in higher education generally show that the first six to seven weeks are crucial for success as this is the period when students establish an academic and social commitment to the university. This is an even more important period for international students as they will also be having to cope with the additional pressures of cultural shock. If the student's family has also come with the student, they will also be in need of support.

It is imperative that universities 'get the welcome right'. This will include things like welcoming students at airports and organising accommodation and introductory social activities, but the student's own department also needs to provide a welcoming environment. Departments have an important responsibility in this area, it is not just the responsibility of the university's international office. For the department, this includes organising a number of induction activities

I used to suffer from my own double perception of myself – the mature, socially functioning person in my native language and the incompetent non-communicator in the target language. Mary Farquhar (1996) expressed this well at a conference when she described how she felt when she was a student in China – 'If you don't have command of the language, you don't have a personality'.

(Nagata, 1999)

79

for the student as well as allocating an individual member of staff who is responsible for the student's general welfare. Most importantly from the department's point of view, this should include appropriate study skills assistance and an introduction to the discipline. The general atmosphere of the department is also important in establishing a welcoming environment for international students, including how support and administrative staff respond to them.

In Manchester, the International Society is open to all university and college international students and runs an active programme of social and cultural events. It also operates the Welcome Scheme which organises for international students to be met at the airport and assists with settling in. The Hospitality Scheme is a host scheme where international students are allocated to a British family and visit their home or go on outings with them.

8.4.2 Try to develop a welcoming ethos in the whole department

- Do international students feel comfortable about approaching the school or departmental office?

- Is it physically and visually welcoming?

- Are front office staff easily physically accessible (are there high barriers separating them from students; do they have to knock on a door or wait for a glass partition to be opened)?

- Are other staff accessible and welcoming?

- Are there posters of other countries, or notices about events in which international students can participate? Are there notices especially of relevance for international students?

- Provide opportunities for social networking such as first year residentials and trips, peer tutoring or mentoring schemes, and social events.

- Arrange for teaching staff with specialist knowledge or experience of the countries or regions from which international students come from, to share their knowledge with other members of staff of how students should be supported.

- Provide contact details of staff and information about specialist support services and encourage students experiencing difficulties to seek assistance early.

Oxford Brookes University is an International University and the School of Hotel and Restaurant Management is an International School. We value cultural diversity in the student body and in our modules and see it as crucial in developing the skills necessary for careers in the Hospitality Industry. We expect all our students to make the most of a wide range of cultures and to develop their ability to communicate effectively with people from different backgrounds.

(Excerpt from School of Hotel and Restaurant Management Field Guide, Oxford Brookes University)

- In course publications and publicity materials, explicitly state that international students are welcome and are valued by the university community.

8.5 Information and support

The importance of accurate information prior to arrival is an important factor in adjustment and acculturation. If universities fail to meet the expectations of international students, problems can be felt more acutely. If high expectations have been created that cannot be fulfilled, the students will experience disappointment and poor adjustment.

International students who have their family with them are likely to adjust more quickly but consideration needs to be given to including the student's spouse in the academic life of their partner, such as by inviting spouses to social events run by the university.

The most significant problems that international students report, however, are academic ones. In a survey of international students at Oxford Brookes University in 1995 (Ames, 1996), 38 per cent of students reported that their most significant problem was academic difficulties, 16 per cent said English language problems, 12 per cent said finances, and 11 per cent said mixing with home students. Further, academic problems peaked in the second year of their studies, and continued through later years. These problems included coping with the content of the course and adapting to different study methods. These findings reinforce the importance of adapting course content and teaching methods to the specific needs of international students to ensure their academic success, throughout their courses.

- Ensure that accurate information is available to international students prior to departure.

- Try to assist students to develop social networks and to join cultural and other support groups.

- Pair students with home students for support and advice.

- Take an interest in international students' personal well-being, and enquire about their progress.

- Provide social activities for international students that include their family members.

One strategy that we use works really well. When an international student has been accepted on to one of our courses, but before they arrive, I set up a link with either a current student or an alumnus from the same country. The prospective student is then able to ask all the questions they would not like to ask us – what shall I bring with me, what shall I wear, what is the food like and so on. I have found this a great success with students from China to South Africa and long-lasting networks are created.

(Lecturer, School of Arts. Publishing and Music, Oxford Brookes University)

- Refer students to specialist support services (such as International Student Advisers) and counselling services (including outside support services run by specific cultural groups) early, before problems become overwhelming for students.

- Ensure that timetabling of lectures, seminars, exams and practical placements or field trips makes allowance for major religious festivals and holidays. Students of particular religious groups often request that classes or exams are not scheduled on particular days or at particular times, e.g. during Muslim and Jewish holidays or during prayer time.

- Be alert for early signs of trouble and take action more quickly than you would for a home student.

The University of British Colombia provides a wealth of information to international students before they arrive. It has established a special website http://www.international.ubc.ca which provides a range of information, including a Pre-Arrival Guide giving information on accommodation, information for students who are bringing their families, and details of orientation programmes (which are mandatory, and students can register prior to their arrival). Students can even register in advance to have a telephone service connected so that it is ready when they arrive. Academic advisers are available within faculties to assist international students with academic problems and study skills and the University runs a peer programme where international students are matched with Canadian students.

Useful cultural information

9

One of the sources of tensions for teachers in working with international students is the fear of creating offence when they are unaware of cultural practices and beliefs. Although it is not possible to be fully aware of all of the taboos or practices of your international students, it is useful to learn about the typical areas of difference, so that you can not only avoid creating offence, but can show a respect for and appreciation of your students' cultural heritage. Above all, the best approach is to try to discover, by contact with your students, information about their backgrounds and beliefs.

9.1 Cultural practices and taboos

All cultures have taboos, and you will encounter students whose taboos are different from your own. Taboos around issues such as contact with the opposite sex, alcohol, contact with certain animals (e.g. pigs or domestic pets, especially dogs), and manual work, may inhibit international students' practical work in the laboratory or in field work or practical placements. Attitudes to animals vary between cultures and many cultures do not afford any special position to animals, such as having them as pets. Sensitivity needs to be exercised with the choice of topics for assignments or case studies, e.g. avoid using a brewery for a case study. On the other hand, it's impossible to list or predict all areas which will cause offence. It's far more helpful to create a climate where you can ask the students if a topic or activity will cause difficulties. Interestingly, one of the key things that may prevent this is the British taboo of asking direct personal questions of the other person.

Personal space is different for different cultures – Middle Eastern students, for example, have small personal space. In some cultures an averted gaze is a mark of respect, which contrasts with the Western belief that this displays untrustworthiness.

Table 9.1	
Examples of confronting behaviours in western and other cultures	
Western cultures	Other cultures
Boasting	Using the left hand, especially for eating or passing objects
Talking loudly	
Asking overly personal questions	Pointing your foot or sole towards a person, or crossing your legs
Standing too close	
Physical contact between the same sex	Beckoning with the index finger or with the palm upwards
Showing too much deference	Pointing, raising the voice, sitting on desks, touching the head
Receiving or giving gifts as inducements	
Spitting or loudly clearing the throat	Opening gifts in public
	Wearing revealing clothing

Lack of sensitivity towards overseas students or to British students from other cultural backgrounds is often due to lack of knowledge about other cultures. Very often there are misunderstandings over verbal and non-verbal communication. Inappropriate language (because different students are not aware of each others social conventions) can create barriers. For example, the lack of use of 'please' and 'thank you' by some students is not a deliberate attempt to be rude or blunt, but simply that the equivalent words just don't exist in some languages...Non-verbal communication can also be misinterpreted. Whereas in some cultures the use of eye contact is a sign of listening behaviour, in others lack of eye-to-eye contact is a sign of respect for the person with whom they have contact.

(Talbot, 1999: 45)

9.2 Improving your sensitivity

In all cultures, certain actions or behaviours are considered either acceptable or unacceptable, and even sometimes disrespectful or threatening. These actions can be confronting or cause discomfort to those who are unfamiliar with them, but it is useful to remember that this is true for all those witnessing new or unexpected behaviours. It is important to realise that this discomfort can occur on both sides and mutual sensitivity is needed to try to avoid causing unintentional offence. Table 9.1 gives some examples of what may be considered confronting in different cultures.

9.3 Religion

People may leave many aspects of their culture behind but all believers take their religion with them when they travel. If study requirements or activities impede or deride their beliefs, this can be distressing and confronting for some international students. Care needs to be taken in allocating students to practical placements, practical activities and in allocating essay or assignment topics or case studies where religious issues may be sensitive. Language used by teachers should not deride other religious beliefs or practices, and if these are being discussed in class, it is important to include materials that have been written or created by people from within those religions themselves. Sensitivity needs to be given also in the timetabling of exams and practical placements to avoid important religious periods.

- Get to know students and ask them how you might together include their religious requirements in their university experience and requirements.

- Be sensitive when setting essay or practical tasks that they do not interfere with taboos around for example alcohol or certain animals.

- Accord respect to other religions when discussing them in class.

- Use materials created by people from within that religion when discussing the religion in class.

- Make sure that prayer rooms are available for Muslim students.

- Do not make assumptions about people who dress differently.

- Make allowances for students if they have to fulfil some kind of outside requirement due to their religion.

Ghena, an Australian-born Muslim woman of Lebanese descent, commented that when she visited Lebanon she was called 'the Australian', but that when she was in Australia her wearing of the headscarf (hijab) meant that she was not regarded as a 'real' Australian. People assumed that she would not be able to speak English. At university she was treated as a 'novelty', with teachers sometimes singling her out with comments such as 'You did really well.' She found this strange as she had been top of her high school, and had now reached final year in Law School without any particular academic difficulties. For Ghena, being Muslim was the most important part of her life, so that the lack of a prayer space at the Law School was a real problem for her. On the other hand, she appreciated being allowed to work on aspects of Islamic law. She was critical of the fact people made assumptions about her on the basis of her costume, without knowing anything about her as a person. She suggested that women wearing the hijab were often assumed to be hostile to all feminist thinking, or to be victims of oppression at home. Ghena's treatment by some of her (often well-meaning) fellow-Australians provided a good example of the pervasive ethnocentrism noted by Volet and Ang (1998). (Asmar, 1999)

For some cultures, religion is not just a set of rules, it is their whole way of life. Not to be able to practise one's own religion is not to be living a real life...Not all members of a religion will be equally devout and strict in practising it...For some, being away from home frees them from obligations, for others, their religion provides security in the face of culture shock...Practising their religion can have physical and mental consequences for students. For example, during the thirty days of Ramadan, Muslims abstain from all food (and food preparation), drink and tobacco from dawn to dusk. Muslim students may be tired or irritable in the afternoons during this period.

(UKCOSA training package, 1993)

Further reading

10

Ballard, B. and Clanchy, J. (1997) *Teaching International Students*, IDP Education Australia, Deakin, ACT.

A comprehensive book looking at the range of dilemmas faced by teachers and international students arising from the mismatch of expectations. It offers suggestions for understanding different perspectives and raises a number of scenarios at the end of each chapter to consider how you might respond.

CVCP *Code of Practice on the Recruitment and Support of International Students in UK Higher Education* (2nd edn, CVCP, 1996).

McNamara, D. and Harris, R. (1997) *Overseas Students in Higher Education.* London: Routledge.

A collection of articles on a range of issues including the student experience, teaching and learning issues and cross-cultural communication, written by teachers who have experience in working with international students in the UK and Asia.

Ryan, Y. and Zuber-Skerritt, O. (eds) (1999) *Supervising Postgraduates from Non-English Speaking Backgrounds.* The Society for Research into Higher Education and Milton Keynes: Open University Press.

A very useful publication which includes a number of poignant case studies of international postgraduate students which should be recommended reading for all members of staff supervising international students.

The British Council (1997) *Feeling at Home: A Guide to Cultural Issues for those Working with International Students.* Manchester: The British Council.

Gives useful information on the perspectives of international students as well as information on cultural practices and beliefs.

Bibliography

Ames, M. (1996) *Oxford Brookes: The International Students Experience.*
Oxford: Oxford Brookes University.

Asmar, C. (1999) Scholarship, experience, or both? A developer's
approach to cross-cultural teaching, *IJAD* 4(1): 18–27.

Ballard, B. and Clanchy, J. (1997) *Teaching International Students.*
IDP Education Australia, Deakin, ACT.

Barker, J. (1997) The purpose of study, attitudes to study and staff-
student relationships. In McNamara and Harris, *op. cit.*

Biggs, J. (1999) *Teaching for Quality Learning at University.*
Milton Keynes: Open University Press.

The British Council, (1997) *Feeling at Home: A Guide to Cultural Issues
for those Working with International Students.*
Manchester: The British Council.

Carroll, J. (1999) Internationalising the Curriculum. Internal
publication for one-day conference, *Teaching and Learning with
International Students.* Oxford: Oxford Brookes University.

Cortazzi, M. and Jin, L. (1997) Learning across cultures.
In McNamara and Harris, *op. cit.*

Denicolo, P. and Pope, M. (1999) Supervision and the overseas
student. In Ryan and Zuber-Skerritt *op. cit.*

Errey, L. (1994) Cultural diversity: or who's who in the University?'
in Rust, C and Pye, J. *Diversity Challenge: How to Support the
Learning of an Increasingly Diverse Student Body.*
Oxford: Oxford Brookes University.

Ewing Cook, C. and Sorcinelli, M., (1999) Building multiculturalism into teaching development programs, *AAHE Bulletin* (American Association for Higher Education) 51(7): 3–6.

Felix, U. and Lawson, M. (1994) Evaluation of an integrated bridging course on academic writing for overseas postgraduate students, *Higher Education Research and Development* 13(1): 59–69.

Furnham A. (1997) The experience of being an overseas student. In McNamara and Harris, *op. cit.*

Furnham, A. and Bochner, S. (1986) *Culture Shock. London:* Methuen.

Harris, R. (1995) Overseas students in the UK university system, *Higher Education* 29: 77–92.

Hofstede, G. (1991) *Cultures and Organisations; Intercultural Cooperation and Its Importance for Survival: Software of the Mind.* London: HarperCollins.

Kember, D. and Gow, L. (1991) A challenge to the anecdotal stereotype of the Asian student, *Studies in Higher Education* 16: 117–28.

Ledwith, S., Lee, A., Manfredi, S. and Wildish, C. (1998) *Multi-Culturalism, Student Group Work and Assessment.* Oxford: Oxford Brookes University.

Ledwith, S. and Seymour, D. (forthcoming) *Home and Away: Group Working Experiences of Multicultural and International Business and Management Students – A Preparation for Global Management Careers?* Oxford: Oxford Brookes University.

McNamara, D. and Harris, R. (1997) *Overseas Students in Higher Education.* London: Routledge.

Nagata, Y. (1999) 'Once I couldn't even spell "PhD student" but now I are one!': personal experiences of an NESB student. In Ryan and Zuber-Skerritt, *op. cit.*

O'Donoghue, T. (1996) Malaysian Chinese Students' Perceptions of What is Necessary for their Academic Success in Australia: A Case Study at one University, *Journal of Further and Higher Education* 20 (2): 67-80.

Open University. (1993) *Equal Opportunities Guide to Language and image.* Open University

Richardson, J. (1994) Cultural specificity of approaches to studying in higher education: a literature survey, *Higher Education* 27(4): 417–32.

Ryan, Y. and Zuber-Skerritt, O. (eds) (1999) *Supervising Postgraduates from Non-English Speaking Backgrounds.* The Society for Research into Higher Education and Milton Keynes: Open University Press.

Scollon, R. (1995) Plagiarism and ideology: identity in intercultural discourse, *Language in Society* 24: 1–28.

Todd, E. (1997) Supervising overseas students: problem or opportunity? In McNamara and Harris, *op. cit.*

UKCOSA (1993) *Partners in Discovery: Developing Cultural Awareness and Sensitivity. A Training Video and Trainer's Guide,* UKCOSA (United Kingdom Council for Overseas Student Affairs).